50 SPIRITUAL
APPETIZERS

50 SPIRITUAL APPETIZERS

Compiled & Edited by

Vinod Dhawan

PARTRIDGE
A Penguin Random House Company

To order additional copies of this book, contact
Partridge India
000 800 10062 62
orders.india@partridgepublishing.com

www.partridgepublishing.com/india

Contents

SECTION THREE
DEATH, SURVIVAL

SECTION FOUR
EMPTINESS

SECTION FIVE
EVIL, CORRUPTION, SUFFERING

SECTION EIGHT
INTERNAL, EXTERNAL

SECTION NINE
DESIRE, THOUGHT

SECTION TEN
LOVE, COMPASSION

SECTION ELEVEN
MIND, EGO

SECTION TWELVE
MANIFESTATION, BODY

SECTION THIRTEEN
SCIENCE

Ekam sat, viprah bahudha vadanti

There is a single Truth but the wise
call it by different names.
-Rig-Veda 3000+ BCE

This book is part of the project titled '100 Spiritual Appetizers'. In view of the long delay in getting permissions, it was decided to split the book into two parts of 50 'gems' each. The complete version of the book will be printed when all the 100 permissions have been received.

*   *   *

INTRODUCTION

Exploring the teachings of Saints and Masters has been the joy of my life. This compilation is an attempt to share this joy with the reader. Thanks to the Internet, I have discovered a host of spiritual teachers and explorers in the West also whose meticulous research has opened up new paths in the spiritual field. Short excerpts provided here are mere glimpses of the teachings of the Masters of East and West but can have a powerful impact if the mood is receptive. These can also serve as an introduction to a teacher and, as symbolized in the title of the book, serve as appetizers. For those whose interest is aroused, links are provided for a detailed study. Short bios of the teachers are also provided again with links for more information. The book is divided into 13 sections devoted to different topics and arranged alphabetically. The alphabetical arrangement within the sections is based on the title of the article and not on the name of the teacher. Each section has an intro which gives an inkling of what is to come.

David Godman, a leading authority on Ramana Maharshi, has also written a lengthy online account of his experiences with Nisargadatta Maharaj. When he first came across the book 'I Am That' by Nisargadatta Maharaj, he says, he could not read it. Whenever he tried, he could not read more than a sentence or two, because the few words had such powerful impact on him that he just had to sit down and reflect. I give his example to justify my "appetizers" approach. However, an excerpt from 'I Am That' could not be included as permission to do so was not received.

In fact this book was started as a '100 Spiritual Appetizers' project. Since permissions took long time coming and in some cases were even denied, it was decided to go ahead with '50 Spiritual Appetizers' for which permissions had been received. Splitting the book into two, '50 More Spiritual Appetizers' will be published when all the permissions have been received.

I had been sharing these excerpts with some friends who persuaded me to put them into book form. I am also encouraged by the growing interest in spirituality in the West. The newspapers and the TV might be forecasting doom, but the growing number of today's spiritual leaders have a different tale to tell. I have it on the authority of Jac O'Keefe, Eckhart Tolle and William Wildblood that the Kaliyuga (age of ignorance) is coming to an end. Irish Master Jac O'Keefe, now settled in California, USA, in a video entitled 'The Kali Yuga Age Is Coming To An End' (available on YouTube) says, "There was time, when awakening was the privilege of a few." It is no longer so. "Manifestation is moving into that part of the wheel (totally cyclical) whereby awakening is very possible. It's not as difficult as it is said in the scriptures; it's not such a big deal any more."

Germany born Eckhart Tolle, now settled in Canada, said in an address at Stanford University, California on February 12, 2013, (available on YouTube), "More and more human beings are able to awaken now, I believe that, I know that and I have met many people . . . It is not necessary to do 30,000 hours of meditation or live in an ashram for 30 years . . . Evolution usually occurs in response to a crisis situation, and we now are faced with such a crisis situation. This is why there is indeed an enormous acceleration in the awakening process of our species . . . This new large-scale spiritual awakening is occurring primarily not within the confines of the established religions, but outside of those structures."

In his blog, 'Rejection of the Contemporary World' dated 11 February 2014, William Wildblood says, "I do agree with those who say that we are living in the latter days of the Kali Yuga . . . However the fact that the Kali Yuga is inevitable, as the time of breakdown prior to the dissolution of this world in preparation for a new cycle, is not an excuse to succumb to the prevailing mores and opinions."

Aspects of Truth put in words by the Saints and Masters lead to a sense of wonder and at times bewilderment. The teachings abound in apparent contradictions viewed from one's own background. For instance, one says Guru is necessary for enlightenment; another is certain that it is a hurdle. Both could be true. As George Bernard Shaw put it, "No man ever believes that the Bible means what it says: He is always convinced that it says what he means." So one tends to accept a teaching according to one's own perception, at that moment. Still there are times when any teaching could strike home in moments when one is caught without prejudice.

How is then one to view the hundreds of present spiritual teachings and techniques now available? Which one to adopt and which one to reject? An excellent example is given in which the peak of a mountain is the state of "enlightenment" on which sit the Saints and Masters who have already reached there. From their exalted position they watch the people of the world struggling to come up the mountain. They see them battling conditions in various forests and valleys and out of compassion point out to them a particular route, "This is the way. This is how I came up," says one. Another one shows another path to come up, emphasizing, "This is the best way. This is how I came up," and so on with another and still another. The bewildered man tries out the different paths but not too sincerely, and remains struggling.

Sureshwaracharya, the great disciple of Shankara, says, "That path alone, by following which a man becomes grounded in the knowledge of the real "I-principle", is the right path for him. There is no one single path which suits all alike."

Elaborating on this, Atmananda Krishna Menon of Kerala, India, in his book Atma Darshan, says, "No attempt need be made to reconcile the different prakriyas (methods) with one another. To do so may even be an obstacle in the path of the aspirant. There may be no difficulty if one can carefully discern the point of view underlying each Prakriya. If this is not possible, one need only hold fast to the Prakriya which appeals to one."

In putting together this book I owe many thanks to Jerry Katz of Nonduality Highlights website and Chris Hebard of Stillness Speaks who introduced me to many present day non-duality teachers. Finally this book would not have been possible without the constant goading by my friend, philosopher and guide, Mr M.B. Lal, a retired senior journalist, author and inventor whose weekly inputs and encouragement I acknowledge with gratitude.

Vinod Dhawan
New Delhi, India

* * *

Section One

BHAKTI (DEVOTION), AWARENESS

Mother Meera has a very liberal approach to spirituality. If you have a feeling for the Divine, it is enough. But mantra chanting helps. She makes a very significant point that one doesn't have to have a fixed mantra for meditation. Any mantra that appeals to you at the moment will do. But it should give a strong feeling and be like music flowing from the heart. She cautions against "techniques" of meditation which often engender pride. The best way, she says, is to remember the Divine in everything and to offer everything to the Divine.

In Indian mythology it is said that Ved Vyas, after having composed the Vedas, the 18 Puranas and other valued scriptures was not feeling satisfied. He approached Sage Narada, the celestial attendant of Lord Narayana, to know the reason. Narada told him he had so far indulged in dry intellectual pursuit of knowledge and forgotten the Lord. He advised, "You should write about the glory of Narayana to inspire bhakti (devotion) in people. Completely surrender to the Lord and sing His glories." Narada then explained to him the Path of Divine Love through 84 sutras (aphorisms) which are now known as 'Narada Bhakti Sutras'. His primary point is, by praying and striving for liberation we've really missed the essence of spirituality. What we should be striving for is not liberation, but devotion.

Swami Ramdas teaches that one must have an atmosphere of freedom in which to develop one's nature, independent of all external interference or guidance. By depending always on guidance from without the disciple does not look within and doesn't rely on God who dwells in the heart.

Poonjaji is asking us to check: If I am not the body, nor the senses, the mind or the intellect, all of whose functioning I am witness to, then who am I? His is an excellent, immediate way leading to awareness.

Young Enza Vita also follows a similar method. "Not knowing anything, not searching for anything, understanding that we can't hold on to anything, leaves us with nothing – nothing except our original nature, pure presence/awareness. Everything else is a concept."

* * *

Mother Meera

Mother Meera was born Kamala Reddy on 26 December 1960 in Chandepalle a small village in Nalgonda district of Andhra Pradesh, India. She had her first samādhi, a state of complete spiritual absorption, at the age of six. When she was 12 her uncle Bulgur Venkat Reddy met her for the first time, and immediately recognized in her the girl of his visions. He became convinced that she is the Divine Mother and started to take care of her, allowing her to unfold her inner experiences.

Mother Meera married a German in 1982. For some years now, she has been giving Darshan (literally *seeing*, primarily in a spiritual context) at Schloss Schaumburg in Balduinstein, a small town in Germany. Mother Meera receives thousands of visitors of all religions for darshan which she conducts in total silence. Her darshan consists of a ritual, where she will touch a person's head, and then look into their eyes. During this process, she reportedly 'unties knots' in the person's subtle system and permeates them with light. She doesn't charge any money for doing so and she will not give lectures.

Contact for details: www.mothermeera.com, email: MotherMeeraFoundation@gmail.com MotherMeeraBookStore@gmail.com

*   *   *

1. Repetition of divine name gives peace and happiness

Mother Meera

Question: Is formal meditation important?

Mother Meera: Yes, to meditate a half an hour or an hour is good. But if one becomes fanatical, wants to leave one's job, live alone and meditate twenty-four hours a day, that is not good.

Q: What kind of meditation should we do?

MM: Close your eyes and sit in silence and do japa on any divine name.

Q: What is japa? Why is it so important?

MM: Japa is the repetition of the name of that in which we believe. Japa is essential. Japa is not simple words – each divine name is full of Divine vibrations. These surround us and protect us and penetrate both our bodies and our whole inner being. Remembrance of the divine name gives immediate peace and happiness and turns us from the worldly to the Divine. There is no special and limited time for japa. It is very good to do japa all day. If this is not possible then remember whenever it is possible. We can practice japa during all activities. It is easier to remember when we do physical work without mental work. This japa helps us to purify our consciousness and make our sadhana easy.

Q: How should we say japa?

MM: Simply. Just say it. In doing japa, one should not strain or try to achieve something specific. One should try to be sincere and to have love of God. The power immediately follows, whether you are aware of it or not.

Q: Would you explain the power of the name?

MM: Each syllable of a divine name – such as Krishna or Jesus – has vibrations which change the atmosphere. Any object that we think about repeatedly generates its own vibration. Even though mantras are strong and powerful, we may not feel the effects immediately but results will come. One can feel the differences in the vibrations of words. Using the word, one can make things change.

Q: Is it necessary to wait for a guru to give a mantra or may one find a mantra on one's own?

MM: Whichever mantra comes to you easily and spontaneously is the one you should do. It should give a strong feeling and be like music flowing from the heart.

Q: I don't have a fixed japa. At different times different forms of the Divine – such as Shiva or Krishna – come into my mind, and I sing the appropriate mantra. Is doing this all right?

MM: Yes, whatever appeals at the moment is all right. One doesn't have to have a fixed mantra.

Q: When I repeat your name is it necessary to say the mantra as given in The Mother, or can I just repeat Mother Meera or simply Meera?

MM: Either is sufficient.

Q: In meditation on a form of the Divine, is it enough to just have the feeling of the Divine, or must one say the mantra as well?

MM: It is enough to have the feeling. But it is good to mentally repeat the name of the Divine as well, because doing this trains the mind and heart.

Q: What is the best technique of meditation?

MM: There are so many techniques. Generally they confuse people. Quite often they increase people's spiritual pride instead of destroying it. The proud man is far from God. You have to be very careful. The best way is to remember the Divine in everything and to offer everything to the Divine.

Q: What is the importance of asking the Divine for something?

MM: If you want anything – love, truth, or courage, for example – you must ask for it. If you ask God for anything humbly and lovingly, you will receive it. But you must ask with your whole heart.

Excerpted from www.mmdarshanamerica.com

* * *

Swami Tadatmananda

Swami Tadatmananda is the founder and resident teacher of Arsha Bodha Center, New Jersey, USA. He was born and brought up in Milwaukee, Wisconsin as a catholic Christian. As he grew up, his interest in Indian Teachings of Vedanta and Upanishads also grew. He pursued a successful career as a software engineer but decided to give up his job and go to India to be with his Guru, Swami Dayananda Saraswati. He was initiated into the Hindu monastic order by his Gurudev on the banks of Ganges in Rishikesh in 1993. Swami Tadatmananda then returned to USA, and set up Arsha Bodha Center, in New Jersey to spread Vedantic Wisdom of Ancient Sages of yore of India to spiritual seekers.

He is a wonderful Sanskrit scholar. The first thing that strikes, when anyone meets Swamiji, is his child-like simplicity and humility. He is ever willing and eager to help spiritual seekers in their Sadhana.

His teachings are full of warmth and humor; his style is informal and personal. He relates easily to all, including teens and children who love to sing bhajans to his guitar accompaniment.

Contact for details: SwamiT@arshabodha.org

* * *

2. Narada's Bhakti Sutra shows bhakti & gyan inseparable

Swami Tadatmananda

There is a common misconception about bhakti. Vedantins think that bhakti is not an intellectual pursuit and conclude, "It's not for me!" But Vedanta is not an intellectual pursuit of knowledge; Vedanta is for spiritual growth. And bhakti is one of the essential practices (sadhana) for spiritual growth.

The idea that there are four separate paths (marga) for spiritual growth (viz. karma; bhakti; dhyana and jnana), and that we can choose only one of them depending on our personality, is a misconception.

It's a mistake to assign ourselves to narrow categories (bhakti for emotional types, jnana for intellectuals, etc). We need them all! Just as for cooking rice, we can't choose among fire, water, and a pot – we need them all.

One reason for studying Narada's Bhakti Sutra is that we need it as an essential sadhana. Secondly, bhakti, properly understood, is not simply intense tapasya as it is depicted in Puranic stories and in movies. In the study of Narada's Bhakti Sutra, we will see inseparability of bhakti and jnanam.

We will see the deeper and more profound meaning of bhakti; more than devotion to God or divine love. At its highest level, bhakti is enlightenment!

It is important to understand that bhakti is not a gradual process that progresses from desire (kama, which is romantic love or sexual attraction) to emotional love (prema) to bhakti. Although, all three have some element of love, they are all completely different from one another.

A good way to understand any absence of a continuum among the three is to consider the metaphor of a seed (kama) giving rise to a tree (prema) and the tree bearing a fruit (bhakti). Although the tree arises from the seed, and the fruit from the tree, the tree and the seed are very different and so are the tree and the fruit.

Tree is not a bigger form of the seed and the fruit is not an intense form of tree. Similarly, bhakti is not an intense form of conventional or emotion based love and emotional love is not physical love or sexual attraction. Physical love is rooted in the physiology of the body like desire for food and water. Emotional love, as between a husband and a wife or between parent and child is located in the mind.

Love has many shades; romantic love is barely love; because it's based on the premise "you make me feel loved, therefore I love you," or, "you make me enjoy life, therefore I love you," or, "I love you as long you love me".

This kind of love is need-based. "I love you" really means in this case, "I need you". On the other hand, love, such as between a mother and a child is a much stronger bond especially when the child is very young. However, parental love is not pure and unconditional, because, there are various expectations.

When the 18-year old wants to be an auto mechanic or a waitress, the parent might disapprove and reject the idea and insist that the child must go to college. In such a case the parent is fulfilling his/her desire, and hence it's not unselfish love.

Essentially, emotional love cannot be pure or totally unconditional, unless one is an enlightened person! Emotional love can be less pure or more pure, but never perfect!

Bhakti, in its highest form, referred to as "parama prema" (supreme love), transcends love; it is limitless and infinite love. No matter how intense the conventional love is, it's not bhakti. Love, either physical or emotional, is based on a sense of incompleteness, a sense of need, however little that need may be.

Bhakti, on the other hand, transcends the mind. It relates to one's true self, which is sat-cit-ananda (eternal, unlimited, consciousness).

Excerpted from September 12, 2006 discourse, Arsha Bodha Center, Somerset, NJ. http://www.arshabodha.org

* * *

Swami Ramdas

Swami "Papa" Ramdas (1884-1963) was born Vittal Rao in the Kerala State of India. As a young man, he was employed as a spinning master in a cotton mill, married in 1908. During his life before renunciation, brief periods of employment were followed by longer periods of unemployment and idleness, affecting both his financial condition and domestic life. For relief from his outer circumstances, he began to chant "Ram," a name of God, which brought him great mental peace and joy. Soon after, his father gave him a holy mantra, and from that point on, his progress and detachment from the material world was quick.

He left his worldly life and began a pilgrimage, taking on the name Ramdas and living on the road in faith. In 1922 he encountered the sage, Ramana Maharshi, and received his grace. In 1931, after years of living on the road in faith, his devotees established Anandashram for him in Kanhangad, Kerala, where he lived with Mother Krishnabai, who also attained the universal vision of God.

They worked to improve the living conditions of the local people, founding a school for the children, establishing a free medical clinic, and setting up a cooperative for weavers.

Contact for details: www.anandashram.org

*　　*　　*

3. For spiritual growth, do not be bound to any institution

Swami Ramdas

There are no external signs to mark out a God-realized saint. He does not grow a horn. But he is always full of bliss. He is happy under all conditions. No miracles can be expected from him, as a matter of course. But they are sometimes done by him by God's will, without his intention to perform them.

Satsang or association with a saint is indeed valuable. But it must be of the right kind. Internal contact must be established. Otherwise there is danger of the aspirant's mind getting externalized and remaining attached to the physical person of the saint, missing the impersonal Truth which the saint embodies. Without reaching the depths of the inner Reality represented by the saint, one cannot reap the full benefits of Satsang.

One must take care not to fall into the error of thinking that a saint's grace can be won by adoring merely his body and serving him without looking upon all beings as his expressions and serving them with an equal vision. There is nothing more dangerous to an aspirant than narrow, personal attitude. His progress depends on the extent to which he is able to expand his heart and universalize his outlook.

One cannot rise beyond a certain stage of spiritual advancement if he is bound to any institution. In spiritual matters, the best rules are those which are not made by others but self-imposed – by the Guru from within. A tree does not grow in the shade of another tree, but gets stunted. It can grow fully only in the open. So also you must have a free and open atmosphere for your spiritual growth.

One may receive light and inspiration from saints and sages, but one must have an atmosphere of freedom in which to develop one's nature, independent of all external interference or guidance. By depending always on guidance from without the disciple does not look within and rely on God who dwells in the heart.

So get inspiration from saints, but do not think of taking shelter permanently in any Ashram. Live alone in a free atmosphere. Then God within will lead you. The indwelling God is none other than your Guru who initiated you from outside as a human being. Guru is the immortal, all-pervading Spirit. Never look upon him as a mere person. If you develop this attitude from the beginning, you will realize that the Guru never dies. You will never feel his absence as he is eternally within you.

Renunciation

It is not by mere external renunciation that one attains God. There are so many who have externally renounced and gone to the forests but have not realized Him. It is not necessary that one should externally renounce anything. It is not the outer condition that matters so much as one's inner state of mind.

If we dedicate our life to God and live in His light, it does not matter where we live. We can live in the family and still realize Him, because God is everywhere and not only in forests and caves. He is in us, with us and all about us. To seek Him, we need not go anywhere.

The examples of Buddha, Chaitanya and Vivekananda are not for all to follow. They are rare cases in which God made them renounce the external ties also so that they might freely serve all mankind. When God wants us to undertake such a glorious mission, by all means, let us not resist the current when it comes to sweep away our narrow limitations. Sri Krishna and Janaka in their lives have shown that even for the work of Lokasangraha, the normal duties of life that fall to our lot need not be abandoned. To attain Moksha for oneself, willful breaking off from external ties is not at all necessary.

Excerpted from 'Thus Speaks Ramdas' published by Anandashram

* * *

H. W. L. Poonja Ji

Hari Wansh Lal Poonja (1910-1997) was born in Gujranwalla, western Punjab, now in Pakistan, in a family of Saraswat Brahmins. His mother was the sister of Swami Rama Tirtha.

At the age of eight he experienced an unusual state of consciousness. He was persuaded by his mother that he could regain this experience by devotion to the Hindu God Krishna, and so he gave himself over to this and began to have visions of Krishna.

Poonjaji married, raised two children and joined the British army, while secretly his love for Krishna and his visions continued. He traveled throughout India asking sages if they could deliver the ability to produce the darshan of God at will.

A sadhu told him that there was a person, Ramana Maharshi, who could show him God. In 1944, when he was 31, he travelled to Tiruvannamalai to meet Ramana Maharshi. Under Ramana's gaze he became aware of the spiritual Heart, which he felt was opening.

Between 1991 and 1997, he settled in Lucknow, Uttar Pradesh, giving satsangs. Thousands of people came to visit him. Many western disciples like Gangaji, Neelam, Mooji owe their awakening to him.

Contact for details: www.satsangbhavan.net

* * *

4. Find out who is the one who sees

'Papaji' (HWL Poonjaji)

Who are you? Where do you come from? Many times you came and many times you returned. You have never attempted to ask yourself who you are. If you had done so, you would never have returned to this miserable samsara. When you have known, this *karma* ceases to function, *samsara* ceases to exist. You return to your original fundamental nature – to Being, to Existence, to Bliss.

That is what you are. That is what you have been. That is what you are going to be. So here is how to do it – it is very easy. Let me introduce you to what is going on here. To begin with, find out who is the one who sees. Ask yourself the question: "Who is the seer?" Find out what is seen. That which is seen is the object and the seer is the subject.

The seer – subject – must be separate from the object, different from the object. *It is that which is seeing the object.* The object is that which is seen. The seer is looking at the object – you are not the object. You may see anything: a horse, a cow, a car, a building, or anything. You are not that. You are the seer.

When you experience your own body you may think that you are the body, but you are not the body. You experience, "I see the body." so you are the seer of the body. It is here that you make the mistake: You become the body and you forget that you are the seer. You have become an object when you say, "I am doing. I am seeing. I am tasting. I am touching. I am smelling. I am hearing."

You have lost your bearings and become the body – the seer is no longer separated from the body. Whatever is seen is an object, so when the body is objectified who is the seer? When you see the body it becomes an object. Whatever you see is an object. If you see your eyes they are objects; if you see your hands they are objects.

What about the mind? You know very well that if your mind is suffering it is not at peace. You know the activities of the mind also. You know, "Now my mind is thinking or not thinking." This means that you are also aware of the activities of the mind. You are something other than the mind. You are not the mind. You are neither the mind nor the body.

The same is true of the working of the senses. When you are working, walking, or talking, you know very well, "I am at work, my hands are working." You know very well that you are not the hand; something else is commanding the hands to work. You are something other than the movement of physical activities. You are not even that.

Now consider the intellect. You decide, "I have to do this. I have to go to Lucknow." You decided and you are here. You guided the intellect to make the decision, "Let's go to Lucknow." then you followed the intellect. So you are guiding even the intellect and you know very well that the intellect is something other than you.

Find out who you are – here and now. You are not the mind. You are not even the *prana* – the breathing. You know very well that breathing is in and out, inhaling and exhaling. You can feel, "I am inhaling, I am exhaling." You know this activity also. Who is watching the inhaling and exhaling? This is all that the body is.

So who are you? You are not all these functions. You will have to ask the question, "Who am I?" This question must be solved but we have postponed it. This is what we have come here to understand, and we have not done this at any time before.

Excerpted from Lucknow Satsang on 6 November,1991 at papajisatsang.com

*   *   *

Enza Vita

Enza Vita was born in a small village in Sicily (Italy) and emigrated to Australia at the age of seventeen. She questioned everything around her, constantly seeking out the point and purpose of our life here on earth. Through a series of deepening awakenings, her search eventually brought her to work in the consciousness community where she became a leader in the personal development movement in Australia, working as editor for *Woman Spirit and Health and Wellbeing* magazines in the 90's, and as editor of *Innerself Newspaper.*

Culminating in a profound spiritual realization in 2007, all her life's work came into a clear, sharp focus, as she began to write and answer questions for those who came to her . . . which eventually became her book, Always Already Free. Enza Vita is the founder of the MahaShanti Foundation, a non-profit organization founded in 2012 to support the awakening of all beings. The organization hosts events throughout Australasia, USA and Europe, publishes books, CDs, and DVDs, and provides access to the teachings online.

Based in Adelaide, South Australia, Enza Vita lives with her partner, Leo Drioli, associate teacher of the MahaShanti Foundation.

Contact for details: www.enzavita.com

* * *

5. You are what you are looking for

Enza Vita

We search for who we are in endless thoughts and imaginings, endless reflections and ideas. This is the search that must be abandoned! We need to surrender all of our cherished concepts, beliefs, and preconceived notions about ourselves. Only when we let go of all ideas of who we *think* we are, are we able to realize what we *truly* are beyond any concept or fleeting experience.

Not knowing anything, not searching for anything, understanding that we can't hold on to anything, leaves us with nothing – nothing except our original nature, pure presence/awareness.

Everything else is a concept, but who you truly are as presence/awareness is not a concept. You are the light illuminating all concepts and everything else. Under no circumstances can you ever leave what you are. You are what you are looking for; you just need to see that it is already here.

There is only Oneness

Awareness is like the sun in the sky. The sun's rays are the pathless path we travel back and forth between our original nature and its expression. Without encountering an object, the light of the sun wouldn't be visible. It is only visible when it reflects back off an object. Manifest reality, the world around us, is the object, a mirror like-reality that reflects back the sun, allowing its light to be seen. Just as a reflection in the mirror, it may look very real, but it is only a reflection. Although it might look like there are two realities, the sun and the mirror, there is really only One.

Thought is awareness in disguise

Our original nature is composed of three qualities:

1. Unending sound or vibration (the sound of our original nature, the heavenly music spoken of in all spiritual scriptures of different religions).
2. Cognizing awareness or luminosity (the ability to perceive even without thought).
3. Unlimited skylike vastness or emptiness (the container allowing for the arising and cognizing of everything)

Because we don't realize our nature, these three qualities become our voices, our thoughts and our physical bodies. As our attention flows to our words and the sounds we make, we forget our original sound. In like manner, our thoughts endlessly come and go, obscuring the unconditioned awareness aspect of our original nature. And as our attention flows out to the physical body, we forget our universal body of unlimited space.

In reality these qualities are present right now in body, speech, and mind, but we don't recognize them because our attention has shifted to the expression of the qualities rather than where the expression is coming from.

All we need do is reverse this flow and realize that we are and have always been what we are searching for. All that has happened is that the attention has moved out into form and identified with it. It's just a case of mistaken identity. Understanding this is the first step, followed by returning the attention to the source of attention and re-stabilizing in it so that attention is not dragged out with every movement of the mind.

Direct self-inquiry

There are two approaches to realizing your true nature. The first is to discover the truth of who you are. The second is to discover what you are not. If you get rid of the false thoughts of who you *think* you are, the remainder is what you *really* are. And when you realize what you really are, all thoughts of who you thought you were drop away and you are free of the suffering of misidentification.

These two approaches are actually the same thing, two ways of expressing the same idea. The famous Indian sage Sri Nisargadatta once said, "You can either push the cart or pull the cart. Both are fine as long as you keep the cart rolling!"

Excerpted from 'Always Already Free' at www.enzavita.com

*   *   *

Section Two
HAPPINESS, PEACE

Lester Levenson made a great discovery. Curious about knowing what caused happiness, he found that when his girl friend declared her love for him, it made him happy. But this feeling did not last. In order for him to have that feeling continuously, she had to continue saying that. As against this, he felt happier when he loved her than when he got that momentary ego-satisfaction when she loved him. Thus Lester concluded that his happiness equated to his loving! If he could increase his loving, then he could increase his happiness!

Swami Nikhilananda Saraswati talks about "holistic success". Some professionals may be greatly praised at work but be utter failures in the family. Some may be good for the family but for society they may be no good. We must be whole individuals. According to him, true success is that which gives joy to me and to others.

Swami Chinmayananda says that modern days of rat race show improvements only on the outside surface. In the absence of a set of values, there can be no happiness for human beings. He finds each one of us searching for happiness in the wrong direction. We will know happiness when we discover the essence of all things, he explains.

Francis Lucille provides a glimpse into his awakening. As the attraction toward the beauty heralded by the Sanskrit chant increased, so did the resistance. As a result of his spiritual search, he says, "the world and its objects had lost their attraction. I was exclusively in love with the Absolute, and this love gave me the boldness to jump into the great void of death, to die for the sake of that beauty."

At the end of the day, everyone wants to return home. Jeff Foster contends this is true in spirituality too. "Creation and destruction, tension and resolution, contraction and release – this is the heartbeat of the cosmos, the heartbeat of all art, music, literature, spirituality, the beat of our very own hearts, which must come to rest eventually," he suggests.

*   *   *

Lester Levenson

Lester Levenson (1909-1994) was born in Elizabeth, New Jersey, USA. In 1952, at age 42, as a physicist and successful entrepreneur, he was at the pinnacle of worldly success, yet he was an unhappy, very unhealthy man. He was so unhealthy, in fact, that after having his second coronary, his doctors sent him home to die.

Instead of giving up, Lester decided to go back to the lab within himself and find some answers. He was able to cut through his conscious mind to find two 'Truths.' The first was that his own feelings were the cause of all his problems. The second was that he had the inborn ability to let go of his feelings. Instead of struggling with them, he discovered how to totally release them.

This put an end to his struggle! He found permanent happiness. He put his discovery into a non-sectarian do-it-yourself system, now called the Sedona Method, which according to the website, "is a process that helps you to change yourself from the inside out by showing you how to eliminate the unconscious blocks that hold you back from having, being and doing what you choose."

Contact for details: www.sedona.com

* * *

6. Happiness is determined by our capacity to love

Lester Levenson

I remembered one evening, a beautiful balmy evening, in the mountains when I was camping with Virginia. We were both lying on the grass, both looking up at the sky, and I had my arm around her. The nirvana, the perfection of the height of happiness was right there. I was feeling how great is love for Virginia! How wonderful is knowing all this nature! How perfect a setting!

Then I saw that it was my loving her that was the cause of this happiness! Not the beauty of the setting, or being with Virginia.

Then I immediately turned to the other side. Boy it was great when she loved me! I remembered the moment when publicly this beautiful, charming girl told the world that she approved of Lester, she loved Lester – and I could feel that nice feeling of approval. But I sensed that it was not as great as what I had just discovered. It was not a lasting feeling. It was just for the moment. In order for me to have that feeling continuously, she had to continue saying that.

So, this momentary ego approval was not as great as the feeling of loving her! As long as I was loving her, I felt so happy. But when she loved me, there were only moments of happiness when she gave me approval.

Days of further cogitation gradually revealed to me that this was correct! I was happier when I loved her than I was when I got that momentary ego-satisfaction when she loved me.

Her loving me was a momentary pleasure that needed constant showing and proving on her part, while my loving her was a constant happiness, as long as I was loving her.

I concluded that my happiness equated to my loving! If I could increase my loving, then I could increase my happiness! This was the first inkling I had as to what brings about happiness. And it was a tremendous thing because I hadn't had happiness. And I said, 'Gee, if this is the key to happiness, I've got the greatest!' Even the hope of getting more and more happiness was a tremendous thing, because this was the number one thing I wanted – happiness.

That started me on weeks and weeks of reviewing my past love affairs. I dug up from the past, incident after incident when I thought I was loving, and I discovered that I was being nice to my girlfriends, trying to get them to love me, and that that was selfish. That was not really love. That was just wanting my ego bolstered!

I kept reviewing incidents from the past, and where I saw that I was not loving, I would change that feeling to loving that person. Instead of wanting them to do something for me, I would change it to my wanting to do something for them. I kept this up until I couldn't find any more incidents to work on.

This insight on love, seeing that happiness was determined by my capacity to love, was a tremendous insight. It began to free me, and any bit of freedom when you're plagued feels so good. I knew that I was going in the right direction. I had gotten hold of a link of the chain of happiness and was determined not to let go until I had the entire chain.

Excerpted from www.sedona.com

*   *   *

Swami Nikhilananda Saraswati

Swami Nikhilananda Saraswati, a spiritual master of the Chinmaya lineage, is the Regional Head of Chinmaya Mission in New Delhi and its centers in Noida, Gurgaon and Faridabad.

Born in Mumbai, Swamiji grew up strongly influenced by the lives and teachings of many saints. It was whilst studying for a Master's degree in Geology, that he developed an interest in spirituality. Thereafter, he studied Vedanta under Swami Tejomayananda, the present head of Chinmaya Mission Worldwide.

Swamiji presents Vedanta as a contemporary science of life, vitally important in a modern world. Having studied the scriptures, Swamiji's persona is a pure reflection of that wisdom.

Swami Nikhilananda has spent more than thirty years reaching out to individuals and groups, bringing about a transformation in their thinking and subsequently in their lives. All those he interacts with – be they students, householders, professionals or corporate leaders, are attracted to his subtlety of thought and his vast experience in sharing this ancient knowledge.

Swamiji has served in Mission centers in India and the U.S. and continues to tour and lecture in many countries.

Contact for details: www.chinmayamissiondelhi.org

*   *   *

7.   Real success lies in making others happy

Swami Nikhilananda Saraswati

Success can be measured from two standpoints – externally and internally. Externally it is the measure of a job well done and the accompanying recognition from society. Internally it is a feeling of achievement, satisfaction, fullness, completeness, wholeness which comes on the completion of a task or the fulfillment of a desire. What is a true measure of success, the outer accolades or the inner joy and peace which is experienced when we know we have performed well?

All of us have various goals which are based on our desires and aspirations. When we fulfill a desire or achieve a goal we feel happy and successful. Till another desire arises and we feel incomplete and we begin to strive again. Sometimes it happens that when we reach a goal we begin to feel a void in our lives and do not know what to do next?

Success can also be measured by the feeling of comfort we have with ourselves. This generally happens when we live according to our intrinsic nature. If we attain what we want and still find something lacking then we know that either our desire was not desirable or the means adopted were not in accordance with nature.

Modern managements feel that if a person is satisfied there will be a lack of motivation, which will work against the interest of the company. This is a negative way of looking at the issue of satisfaction. When a person is positively satisfied, he/she wants to share the feelings of joy and contentment with others, wants to work for the welfare and well being of others. His/her motivational levels are higher and the opposite happens-he/she wants to do even more and work more efficiently.

This is the state of mind of a Mahatma. Swami Chinmayananda, the founder of Chinmaya Mission went all over the world, reaching out to people not because he desired anything. He did it out of a joy of sharing what he had, so that others may benefit as well and share in his knowledge, good fortune and success. It was an expression of the joy he felt within. True success is that which gives joy to me and to others.

Success should include or embrace all aspects of my life – holistic success. Some professionals may be greatly praised at work but be utter failures in the family. Some may be good for the family but for society they may be no good. We must be whole individuals, just as God intended us to be.

We must learn how to share success from the life of Lord Rama. After returning from Lanka he was asked how he won the battle and he gave credit to all those who had helped him, making even the ordinary monkeys great. Real success lies in making others happy and giving credit to the whole team. These are the distinguishing marks of a great or true leader. He carries the team with him.

Why do people want success? Success is associated with fame, reaching the top. It is associated with perfection, wholeness, joy and completeness. Success is an expression of our Self which is Supreme and perfect. Therefore we have this thirst for success because we are that supreme alone.

We want to be great because we are great. It is a natural desire. Everyone wants to be perfect, wants to win, wants to remain ahead of everyone. If we understand all its connotations, then my success will not be dependent on anyone's failure or be gained by pulling someone down.

Excerpted from article 'Formula for Success' www. chinmayamissiondelhi.com

* * *

Swami Chinmayananda

Swami Chinmayananda (1916-1933) born Balakrishna Menon in Kerala, India, was a spiritual leader and teacher who inspired the formation of Chinmaya Mission, a worldwide nonprofit organization, to spread the knowledge of Advaita Vedanta.

During British rule, Balakrishnan's nationalist activities led to his imprisonment. Later, as reporter for The National Herald newspaper, he decided to write an exposé on what he believed to be the bluff of the swamis in the Himalayan regions. To investigate and uncover such veils of alleged sanctity, he travelled to Ananda Kutir, Swami Sivananda's ashram in Rishikesh.

However Balakrishnan's journey to expose others ended up in exposing himself to his own spiritual revolution and evolution. Swami Sivananda's divinity, love, and Vedanta teachings overwhelmed the young skeptic. He was initiated into sannyasa by Swami Sivananda, who then guided him to the most renowned Vedanta master of the time, Swami Tapovanam, who lived in Uttarkashi, in the Himalayas. As his disciple, Swami Chinmayananda led an austere life and underwent an intense study of Vedantic texts.

Swami Chinmayananda is renowned for teaching the ancient Hindu scriptures in a logical and scientific manner. From 1951 onward, he spearheaded a global Hindu spiritual and cultural renaissance that popularized the religion's esoteric scriptural texts, teaching them in English all across India and abroad. His wit and erudition made him a dynamic orator, captivating crowds of up to several thousand in free discourses twice a day for nearly 40 years.

Contact for details: chinmayamission.com

*   *   *

8.   Searching for happiness in the wrong direction

Swami Chinmayananda

Charms of technology have enthralled the public almost as a danseuse will. If we carefully look back on the history of the world, it is clear we are the saddest generation of humanity. But why? The caveman had his laughter and was happy. The modern days of rat race show improvements only on the outside surface. In the absence of a set of values for ourselves how can there be happiness for human living?

The over-development of one cell to the exclusion of others is called cancer in medical terms. The faster development of one facet of civilization irrespective of the other facets is the cancer of modern times. Instincts and impulses rule us. Each one of us is honestly searching for happiness in the wrong direction. Desire after desire is what makes us unhappy.

What is the purpose of existence? There is an infinite variety in nature. Who created this variety? Why? Such questions do not arise in the animal mind. Question, Enquiry, Discovery – this should be our style of living.

Everything is conditioned by Time and Space. BMI is constantly changing. So is FET. At our present level of evolution man cannot observe the world objectively. Einstein himself despaired because of two changing factors. 'Jagat', the universe, itself comes from the root word which means change or flux.

So to the question 'What is unchanging?' you cannot answer from your experience. Only the Rishis can answer.

There exists something which does not change. Who is knowing that everything is changing?

When you watch the roadside traffic, you are the Subject; everything else is the Object. Is there not in you a centre which is observing, knowing and becoming conscious of all changes? If I am also changing I cannot observe the change. If you are part of the system of movement, you cannot be a witness to the movement. But you are conscious that everything is changing. Therefore you must be the changeless.

There exists something in you which is changeless in your BMI. This subjective essence in me is changeless, because it is not conditioned by space and time. This immortal essence, essential 'I' in my true nature, is the pure Consciousness, Light or Awareness. All our experiences are dancing about because of this.

They are all shining because of this Awareness. That which you are not aware of does not exist. That there exists such an essential Reality is the theme of all scriptures. There exists something higher in every one of us. It is called Brahman. That is not a thing in itself. It is represented by AUM. It stands for the changeless centre from which one picks up all his conscious experiences.

Matter is inert (no locomotion) and insentient (no awareness). "I" am also matter but "I" have locomotion and sentience. Therefore there exists something other than matter. In the bulb there exists something other than the bulb which makes it glow. In the steam engine there exists something other than the engine which is propelling it. It is the Power, Shakti. It expresses you in you, me in me, the bird in the bird and the plant in the plant. Life is one.

Excerpted from the speech of Swami Chinmayananda at Chennai on November 7, 1992. The subject was Logic of Spirituality. Source Central Chinmaya Mission Trust, Mumbai

*   *   *

Francis Lucille

Francis Lucille (born 1944 in France) is a spiritual teacher and author currently residing in California. He has been holding dialogues and meditation sessions throughout the world, helping people to abide in their own natural state. Francis gently guides through words and a powerful silence.

After graduating from the École Polytechnique, Paris, in 1966, he worked as a mathematician and physicist.

Francis became a disciple of Jean Klein, a French Advaita teacher whom he met in 1975. This was the beginning of a close association that lasted until the death of his friend and spiritual master in 1998.

With impersonal compassion, Francis gently instructs his students and, by his presence, permits them to witness how universal principles can manifest in the human being. He is humble and makes absolutely no effort to promote his body of work. It is merely available as a service to those desiring further pointers on the path to Self-realization.

Francis gently guides through words and a powerful silence. His teaching is through the direct path in which teachers challenge the traditional belief that long periods of sadhana are needed by anyone seeking truth, since we are already realized.

Contact for details: www.francislucille.com

*   *   *

9.   Peace & understanding prevails at the end of the road

Francis Lucille

There is not a one-size-fits-all path to the truth. The way to the discovery of our true nature varies from one seeker to another. It may be a sudden and dramatic experience or a subtle, seemingly gradual path. The touchstone, in all cases, is the peace and understanding that prevails at the end of the road.

Due to my upbringing by materialistic and antireligious parents and to my training in Mathematics and Physics, I was both reluctant to adopt any religious belief and was suspicious of any nonlogically or nonscientifically validated hypothesis.

I was sitting in silence, meditating in my living room with two friends. It was too early to fix dinner, our next activity. Having nothing to do, expecting nothing, I was available. My mind was free of dynamism, my body relaxed and sensitive, although I could feel some discomfort in my back and in my neck.

After some time, one of my friends unexpectedly began to chant a traditional incantation in Sanskrit, the Gayatri Mantra. The sacred syllables entered mysteriously in resonance with my silent presence which seemed to become intensely alive.

I felt a deep longing in me, but at the same time a resistance was preventing me from living the current situation to the fullest, from responding with all my being to this invitation from the now, and from merging with it. As the attraction toward the beauty heralded by the chant increased, so did the resistance, revealing itself as a growing fear that transformed into an intense terror.

At this point, I felt that my death was imminent, and that this horrendous event would surely be triggered by any further letting go on my behalf, by any further welcoming of that beauty. I had reached a crucial point in my life.

As a result of my spiritual search, the world and its objects had lost their attraction. I didn't really expect anything substantial from them. I was exclusively in love with the Absolute, and this love gave me the boldness to jump into the great void of death, to die for the sake of that beauty, now so close, that beauty which was calling me beyond the Sanskrit words.

As a result of this abandon, the intense terror which had been holding me instantaneously released its grip and changed into a flow of bodily sensations and thoughts which rapidly converged toward a single thought, the I-thought, just as the roots and the branches of a tree converge toward its single trunk.

In an almost simultaneous apperception, the personal entity with which I was identifying revealed itself in its totality. I saw its superstructure, the thoughts originating from the I-concept and its infrastructure, the traces of my fears and desires at the physical level.

Now the entire tree was contemplated by an impersonal eye, and both the superstructure of thoughts and the infrastructure of bodily sensations rapidly vanished, leaving the I-thought alone in the field of consciousness. For a few moments, the pure I-thought seemed to vacillate, just as the flame of an oil lamp running out of fuel, then vanished.

At that precise moment, the immortal background of Presence revealed itself in all its splendor.

Excerpted from Eternity Now by Francis Lucille. www. francislucille.com

*   *   *

Jeff Foster

Jeff Foster belongs to a younger generation of non-duality teachers and is influenced by Advaita, Sufism and Zen. He graduated in astrophysics from Cambridge University in 2001 and "awoke from the dream of separation" after two years of searching. Jeff has his base in the UK, but he travels extensively in both Europe and the United States to give meetings and seminars.

In his mid-twenties, after a long period of depression and illness, he became addicted to the idea of 'spiritual enlightenment' and embarked on an intensive spiritual quest for the ultimate truth of existence.

The spiritual search came crashing down with the clear recognition of the non-dual nature of everything, and the discovery of the extraordinary in the ordinary. In the clarity of this seeing, life became what it always was: intimate, open, loving and spontaneous, and Jeff was left with a deep understanding of the root illusion behind all human suffering, and a love of the present moment.

> Jeff presently holds meetings, retreats and private one-to-one sessions around the world, gently but directly pointing people back to the deep acceptance inherent in the present moment.
>
> *Contact for details: www.lifewithoutacentre.com*

*   *   *

10. Home is not a place, thing or person – it is rest

Jeff Foster

The search for home goes so very, very deep in the human psyche. Perhaps it motivates everything we do. Throughout all human history, this search has expressed itself in every single facet of our lives – in our art, our music, our science, our mathematics, our literature, our philosophy, in our quest for love, in our spirituality.

Male and female seek each other, try to complete themselves through romantic or sexual union. We seek our 'soul mates', search for our 'other halves' who will complete us. In our cosmic homesickness we seek union with God, with Spirit, with Nature, with the holy guru. We buy houses together and magically transform them into homes, and after a long, exhausting day at kindergarten or at the office, we just want to go home, back to mother, back to our loved ones, back to sleep, back to the cosmic womb.

We populate landmasses, create countries, and call them our homelands, our motherlands, our fatherlands. We fight and die to protect our homelands – the lands we love, the lands our ancestors were born in and died in. We wander in the wilderness for a thousand years and long for the promised land, for our heaven on earth, for our Jerusalem.

Characters in novels, in plays, in movies, journey far away from home, discover who they really are, and return home, or find a new home. They are somehow changed, somehow the same. We love our movies, our television shows, to end with a tearful homecoming or reunion, and the story of the one who never came home haunts us like anything.

In The Wizard of Oz, perhaps our most beloved movie of all time, a young girl leaves her sepia-tinted home, goes on an incredible, colorful journey, meets various facets of herself to befriend or defeat, and returns home, to the same place – but now she sees what's really there.

In Disney musicals, often the main character, feeling like an outcast in their own home, will sing a song about their longing for adventure, for love. Something calls them away from home, but in the end, they return home, or they find a new home, their true home, their true place in the world.

It has been suggested that on the most basic level every story, every myth, shares this common structure – ending with the hero's return. As children, we are homesick when we are away from home for too long, away from the ones we love.

In music, notes and chords go on a similar journey, moving away from home, creating tension for the listener, but finally they resolve themselves, and we feel like the song moved us in some way – took us on a journey away from the ordinary, and returned us to where we were, somehow changed, touched, transformed.

In art, the interplay of foreground and background, light and shade, positive and negative space creates tension, drama. Our longing for resolution makes the artwork compelling. Perhaps it is the same longing that has driven mathematicians, philosophers, physicists, for all of human history, to seek some kind of grand, unified, all-encompassing theory of reality, to find wholeness in the chaos, to find love in the midst of devastation.

The spiritual seeker leaves home in search of enlightenment, and returns home again, only to discover that the enlightenment she sought was there from the beginning. When people die we say they have 'gone home', or found a new home where they can rest eternally. We are told that even the universe is expanding and contracting – somehow seeking equilibrium, seeking home.

Yin and yang, light and dark, creation and destruction, tension and resolution, contraction and release – this is the heartbeat of the cosmos, the heartbeat of all art, music, literature, spirituality, the beat of our very own hearts, which must come to rest eventually. All things long to come to rest. It is no wonder that at its root the word 'home' means 'rest' or 'lie down'.

Home is not a place, a thing, or a person – it is rest.

Excerpted from http://www.deepestacceptance.com

*   *   *

Section Three

DEATH, SURVIVAL

O ld age is the ideal time to prepare for death. One is now psychologically ripe for this great endeavor. Douglas Harding says if you deny or actively resist your built-in need to devote much of the energies of the closing decades of your life to that goal, you are likely to be unhappy for no outwardly discernible reason, deeply afraid of what's to come. You have now all the experience of life you need in order to make sense of it. "What more fitting task therefore — what more urgent duty — awaits you than this one: assemble the jigsaw puzzle of your life till the master-design suddenly takes shape."

Gangaji says to be willing to tell the truth is to risk losing everything. In the commitment to the discovery of the complete truth, there has to be a ruthless examination as to where we lie. What has to be faced is what you think the truth of yourself is, and how you have lied to yourself to cover it up. "Are you willing to tell the truth all the way down to the depths? Are you willing to lay bare what your life is really about, where your attention really is in the name of enlightenment or peace? Are you willing to be humbled by seeing the mechanism that is really running underneath prayers for enlightenment and peace?" Read on to find out.

Swami Vivekananda says the most stupendous wonder in human life is the inability of our mind to conceive our own annihilation, in spite of deaths all around. "Even to imagine my own annihilation I shall have to stand by and look on as a witness." There is something in us which is free and permanent. But it is not the body; neither is it the mind. He points out to a freedom that in spite of the colorings of name and form, is ever asserting its unshackled existence.

* * *

Douglas Harding

Douglas Harding was born in 1909 in Suffolk, England into the Exclusive Plymouth Brethren, a community in which newspapers, novels, theatres, cinemas and even laughter were forbidden or frowned upon. Studying architecture in London at the age of 21 he confronted the Elders with his objections and was promptly excommunicated.

Harding began practicing architecture in London and later in India, where he was commissioned into the Royal Engineers during the Second World War. But all this time he was driven by the burning question "Who am I?"

A key moment in his enquiry was discovering a drawing by the Austrian physicist and philosopher Ernst Mach. It was a self-portrait, but not as seen in a mirror. Mach had drawn what he actually saw from where he was – feet, legs, hands, arms and torso – but no face or head. Harding realized that this was how he saw himself if he looked objectively. It was like having the universe on his shoulders instead of a head.

In the late 1960s and 1970s Harding developed awareness exercises to make it easy to see one's headlessness and to explore its meaning and implications in everyday life.

Contact for details: http://www.headless.org

* * *

11. Coming to terms with your own death

Douglas Harding

Long before we reach our teen our ability to pick up a language has hugely deteriorated. At twenty or so our table tennis starts falling off, at twenty-five our figure skating and gymnastics, at thirty our football or tennis. However, our ability to play chess or run a business or make a speech or write or paint or compose may well have been growing all the time and perhaps we've only just begun to do philosophy in any disciplined or creative fashion. And so on, gaining skills and losing skills all the way up to – well, up to what age?

While there's still life there's still the question: 'What to do now' what's the right job for me, what do I enjoy most, at this time of my life? Which leads to: 'what – if anything – can I do as well now as in my fifties and sixties? Or even – is it possible? – better than then, provided I keep up the needful practice? In short, what's appropriate now?'

It's not for nothing that, traditionally, wisdom is expected to come with age, that the Sage is generally pictured as an Ancient Sage, that the Wise Old Man is among the more convincing of Jung's archetypes. I'm certainly not suggesting that enquiry into your essential Nature and destiny – into the great questions of life and death – is best put off till hoary old age, which has all too obvious reasons for specializing in such weighty (not to say heavy) matters. On the contrary, the enquiry can't begin too early in life. What I am saying is that – even if you've left it rather late – this is just the job for you to pursue now, through old age to very old age. It's exactly what you have an excellent chance of becoming very good at indeed. And this for a variety of reasons.

It's likely you have now either realized your ambitions and find yourself as unsatisfied as ever, or else you have given them up as unrealistic or unachievable. In either case you are being helped towards that measure of detachment which is just what's now needed.You have all the leisure free from pressing duties and responsibilities, which you could want for this, the most engrossing of all the enterprises of your life.

According to Carl Jung (and all the evidence I have suggests he's right) you are now psychologically ripe for this great endeavor – which is coming to terms with your own death, and (much more than that) having death itself as your goal. On the other hand, if you deny or actively resist your built-in need to devote much of the energies of the closing decades of your life to that goal, you are likely to be unhappy for no outwardly discernible reason, deeply afraid of what's to come perhaps clinically sick.

You now have in the bag all the raw material, all the loose pieces of information, all the experience of life you need in order to make sense of it. What more fitting task therefore – what more urgent duty – awaits you than this one: assemble the jigsaw puzzle of your life till the master-design suddenly takes shape: enabling you to look back on the those once so poignant and absorbing concerns as trivial in themselves, yet revealed as indispensable now they are subordinated, to the great concerns: What's it all in aid of? What, above all, is my true identity, and therefore my true role and fate? Am I made of god and accordingly indestructible; or am I made of the less hardwearing stuff and accordingly soon for the cosmic dump where everything that is not God ends up?

Excerpted from 'The Little Book of Life and Death', Chapter 13; The Ascent

* * *

Gangaji

Gangaji was born Merle Antoinette Roberson in Texas in 1942 and grew up in Mississippi. After a divorce she sought to change her life via political activism and spiritual practice. She took Buddhist Bodhisattva vows, practiced Zen and Vipassana meditation, helped in a Tibetan-style meditation center, and began a career as an acupuncturist in the San Francisco Bay area. But she felt unfulfilled by her seemingly successful life.

Meanwhile Eli Jaxon-Bear, who had become her second husband, met Papaji in India. Struck by the letters she received from Eli, Gangaji herself traveled to Lucknow, India to meet Papaji in 1990. In her autobiography *Just Like You* she wrote, "The extraordinary event in this life was that I met Papaji. Until then I looked everywhere for the transcendental or the extraordinary, but after meeting Papaji I began to find the extraordinary in every moment." Papaji gave her the name Gangaji, and asked her to share what she had directly realized with others.

Gangaji currently writes and tours as a teacher. She holds that the truth of who you are is already free and at peace, which can be realized simply by ending one's search.

Contact for details: www.gangaji.org

* * *

12. Lying is a major part of survival

Gangaji (Merle Antoinette Roberson)

As humans we are trained to lie. Lying is a major part of survival. To be willing to tell the truth is to risk losing everything. When you have made a choice to be committed to the truth, then the truth is a ruthless master. That commitment will expose every aspect of hiding and every justification of that hiding.

In the commitment to the discovery of the complete truth, there has to be a ruthless examination as to where we lie. What has to be faced is what you think the truth of yourself is, and how you have lied to yourself to cover it up. In discovering what it is we are denying, there can be a space – a space that is the conduit for discovering the deepest truth.

First you have to tell the truth about what is truly wanted. What do you really want? Freedom and enlightenment? Really? Tell the truth. If you get freedom or enlightenment, what will that give you? Perhaps the answer is, "It will give me respect, or lovability, or fame, or eternal happiness, or power, or relief from the suffering of the world." In telling the truth you can discover what is actually wanted. You discover what you want enlightenment to supply you with. It is often not a pretty truth, but it is necessary to reveal it to yourself.

That is not the end. There is more. If you are willing to tell the truth about what fame, or lovability, or power will give you, you get to the desire underneath that: It may be something like, "Everybody will love me," or "People will finally see who I am and give me what I want." And if you tell the truth about what *that* will give you, then you start to get close to what the essential yearning really is.

Are you willing to tell the truth all the way down to the depths? Are you willing to lay bare what it is your life is really about, where your attention really is in the name of enlightenment or peace? Are you willing to be humbled by seeing the mechanism that is really running underneath prayers for enlightenment and peace? This is the opportunity to meet the abyss; the huge hole that most avoid throughout life, the intimation that really you are worse than worthless, that you are nothing at all.

If you are sincere in your intention to really know the truth, and if you are willing for that knowing of the truth to give you nothing but itself – no fame, no recognition, no happiness, no release, no universal love – if you want the truth that badly, then you are willing to fall into the abyss; to meet the abyss with your full attention; to meet the truth that you are nothing.

The invitation is to just drop through all the lies. Drop your consciousness through them. Feel the burn, the pain, the ache, the horror, the delusion, the lie and the temptation to cheat with more soothing lies. "My God, I'm worse than all of that . . . worse than nothingness." And *there* is the secret, the great revelation.

Meeting the abyss is the full circle. It is coming home, coming back to yourself. The extraordinary report that everyone who has met that abyss brings back to you is that the nothingness you are is awake, alive consciousness. Awake, alive consciousness, and in love. No-thingness is everything you have been looking for in defining yourself as somebody worth something, or somebody worthless. Everything you have been seeking is right here in the depth of your being, under all the lies. It is what has been both sought and fled from all along! It is the simplicity and purity of who you are, here now and always.

Excerpted from www.gangaji.org

*   *   *

Swami Vivekananda

A spiritual genius of commanding intellect and power, Swami Vivekananda crammed immense labor and achievement into his short life, 1863-1902. Born in the Datta family of Calcutta, the youthful Vivekananda embraced the agnostic philosophies of the Western mind along with the worship of science.

At the same time, vehement in his desire to know the truth about God, he questioned people of holy reputation, asking them if they had seen God. He found such a person in Sri Ramakrishna, who became his master, allayed his doubts, gave him God vision, and transformed him into sage and prophet with authority to teach.

After Sri Ramakrishna's death, Vivekananda renounced the world and criss-crossed India as a wandering monk. His mounting compassion for India's people drove him to seek their material help from the West. Accepting an opportunity to represent Hinduism at Chicago's Parliament of Religions in 1893, Vivekananda won instant celebrity in America and a ready forum for his spiritual teaching.

For three years he spread the Vedanta philosophy and religion in America and England and then returned to India to found the Ramakrishna Math and Mission. Exhorting his nation to spiritual greatness, he wakened India to a new national consciousness.

Contact for details: www.belurmath.org/

* * *

13. Two wonderful facts of life: Death & Freedom

Swami Vivekananda

In the great Sanskrit epic, the Mahabharata, the story is told how the hero, Yudhishthira, when asked by Dharma to tell what was the most wonderful thing in the world, replied, that it was the persistent belief of mankind in their own deathlessness in spite of their witnessing death everywhere around them almost every moment of their lives.

And, in fact, this is the most stupendous wonder in human life – the inability of our mind to conceive our own annihilation. Even to imagine my own annihilation I shall have to stand by and look on as a witness.

Although it is perfectly true that when the human mind transcends its own limitations, it finds the duality reduced to an indivisible unity; on this side of the unconditioned, the whole objective world – that is to say, the world we know – is and can be subject, and therefore, before we would be able to conceive the annihilation of the subject we are bound to conceive the annihilation of the object.

So far it is plain enough. But now comes the difficulty. I cannot think of myself ordinarily as anything else but a body. My idea of my own permanence includes my idea of myself as a body. But the body is obviously impermanent, as is the whole of nature – a constantly vanishing quantity.

Where, then, is this permanence?

There is one more wonderful phenomenon connected with our lives, without which 'who will be able to live, who will be able to enjoy life a moment? – the idea of freedom.

This is the idea that guides each footstep of ours, makes our relations to each other – nay, is the very warp and woof in the fabric of human life. But then what is free? The body, or even the mind? It is apparent to all that they are as much bound by law as anything else in the universe.

Now the problem resolves itself into this dilemma: Either the whole universe is a mass of never-ceasing change and nothing more, irrevocably bound by the law of causation, not one particle having a unity of itself, yet is curiously producing an in-eradicable delusion of permanence and freedom – or, there is in us and in the universe something which is permanent and free, showing that the basal constitutional belief of the human mind is not a delusion.

It is the duty of science to explain facts by bringing them to a higher generalization. Any explanation, therefore, that first wants to destroy a part of the fact given to be explained, in order to fit itself to the remainder, is not scientific, whatever else it may be.

So, any explanation that wants to overlook the fact of this persistent and all-necessary idea of freedom, commits the above-mentioned mistake of denying a portion of the fact, in order to explain the rest, and is therefore, wrong.

The only other alternative possible, then, is to acknowledge, in harmony with our nature, that there is something in us which is free and permanent.

But it is not the body; neither is it the mind. The body is dying every minute. The mind is constantly changing.

The body is a combination, and so is the mind; and as such can never reach to a state beyond all change. But beyond this momentary sheathing of gross matter, beyond even the finer covering of the mind is the Atman, the true Self of man, the permanent, the ever-free.

It is his freedom that is percolating through layers of thought and matter, and, in spite of the colorings of name and form, is ever asserting its unshackled existence. It is his deathlessness, his bliss, his peace, his divinity that shines out and makes itself felt in spite of the thick layers of ignorance.

This article was originally published in the New York Morning Advertiser (now defunct) under the title 'Is the Soul Immortal.'

*   *   *

Section Four
EMPTINESS

Consciousness is commonly viewed as the foundational reality of everything. But, Susan Kahn argues, this perspective does not recognize consciousness as dependent upon other phenomena to appear. "Consciousness must be conscious of something to be considered conscious. If there is no content to be conscious of, how could consciousness be recognized as being conscious? When it is seen that consciousness depends upon other things, then consciousness can also be seen as empty." As there is no inherently existent consciousness, there is no inherently existent "me." This implies that there is no ultimate identity to defend, or need to desperately grasp and cling to the "mine."

When we or someone dear to us has an accident or gets seriously ill, it's as if blinders have been removed from our eyes. We see the meaninglessness of so much of what we do and the emptiness of so much we cling to. Pema Chödrön says when her mother died, she found boxes of papers and trinkets that she treasured, things that she held on to. They had represented security and comfort for her. "The loss of my mother and the pain of seeing so clearly how we impose judgments and values, prejudices, likes and dislikes, onto the world, made me feel how we were making much ado about nothing and suffering from it tremendously."

The Heart Sūtra is considered the best-known and most popular Buddhist scripture. In a commentary on it, Geshe Lama Konchog says the mind or consciousness posited this physical form, and because the physical form appears to the mind, it therefore lacks inherent, or true, existence. By having an understanding of the impermanence of physical form, we can eliminate the thought of eternalism. When we say that things do not exist inherently, it shows the nominal existence of conventional existence.

*   *   *

Susan Kahn

Susan Kahn is a licensed psychotherapist in California who unites both traditional and non-dual emptiness teachings. She completed her graduate degree at a University in California, with high honors. She explains her passion for the teaching and work as a therapist, as wanting to penetrate the surface of things and to help others.

Her background is from the tradition of Buddhist emptiness teachings. In this teaching, nothing is seen to exist separately, but to be interrelated and interdependent at every turn. She claims Emptiness teachings, both east and west, are powerful in freeing oneself from a life of fragmentation, conflict, and from the fear that is integral to the sense of being a separate self in a world of separate people and things. As a practicing psychotherapist, she

> combines traditional psychological insight and methods
> with emptiness teachings.
>
> *Contact for details: emptinessteachings.com & emptinesscafe.com*

14. Consciousness is empty, and so is love

Susan Kahn

From the perspective of emptiness teachings, to say
that something is empty means that it is empty of inherent
existence. Instead, everything exists interdependently like
fire and fuel. Deconstructing consciousness and seeing its
emptiness takes examination, but is profoundly liberating.
For the idea of consciousness as its own thing perpetuates
the sense of an inherently separate self.

Consciousness is commonly viewed within non-
duality, as pure consciousness and as the foundational
reality of everything. This perspective does not recognize
consciousness as dependent upon other phenomena to
appear, but is seen as self-created.

However, this argument runs into a problem. In order
to create or produce itself, consciousness would need to have
already existed!

Consciousness is also said to be conscious of itself. But
for consciousness to indivisibly know itself is a muddled
notion. Consciousness must be conscious of something
to be considered conscious. If there is no content to be
conscious of, how could consciousness be recognized as
being conscious? When it is seen that consciousness depends

upon other things, then consciousness can also be seen as empty.

Furthermore, for consciousness to be conscious of itself, would require it to have an interior, making the claim that consciousness is an indivisible unity, impossible. It would take time and space for consciousness to be conscious of itself.

Furthermore, when consciousness is viewed as inherently existent, it must be changeless. However, whatever is unchanging must be inherently dead, isolated from the flow of interrelational continuation.

Alternatively, consciousness can be viewed as existing interdependently, as non-dual inter-reflections, all empty of their own essence. This interdependence can manifest very subtly, as in non-conceptual meditative states.

Buddhist teachings make the additional argument that consciousness is dependent upon what is not considered conscious. We are conscious of something, we recognize something that we would call non-conscious elements. And because consciousness does not exist solely as itself, it can function throughout the world.

Furthermore, consciousness is dependent upon a body, including the senses. So what sort of pure consciousness can this really be? What intrinsic property can consciousness truly hold?

How can anything be both fundamentally separate and connected? Instead of existing separately, it can be observed that consciousness is a mutually dependent phenomenon, just as fire does not burn itself and is utterly dependent upon fuel.

Consciousness appears to exist in a self-created, self-powered way. It is assumed that consciousness operates itself, but this is no more so than trees that are blowing, themselves intend to blow. Consciousness is an interrelated movement of form, but is treated as if it is altogether privileged.

In emptiness teachings, it is said that there is an equality among all phenomena because nothing can be truly separated out. This expands the meaning of love and compassion. Yet, this is not to say that there exists an autonomous, undifferentiated loving unity either.

Love and compassion depend upon a relative otherness to be loving and compassionate toward. For love does not love itself. We don't consider an act of love to be self-referring, just as consciousness must be conscious of what is not considered consciousness.

And as consciousness involves diversity, love is also of the world. As everything exists without their own essence, things are neither the same nor different from each other, as nothing exists separately.

And too, as there is no inherently existent consciousness, there is no inherently existent "me." This implies that there is no ultimate identity to defend, or need to desperately grasp and cling to the "mine."

This lightens suffering. For as everything interrelates, there is no place to fall. Such understanding opens the heart to seeing unity within diversity, while embracing the diversity within unity. Fear, intolerance and other afflictions, cannot securely withstand such a great embrace.

Excerpted from: http://www.emptinessteachings.com

*   *   *

Pema Chödrön

Pema Chödrön (born Deirdre Blomfield-Brown in 1936) is a notable American figure in Tibetan Buddhism. A disciple of Chögyam Trungpa Rinpoche, she is an ordained nun, author, and teacher in the Shambhala Buddhist lineage Trungpa founded.

A prolific author, she has conducted workshops, seminars, and meditation retreats in Europe, Australia, and throughout North America. She is resident and teacher of Gampo Abbey, a monastery on Cape Breton Island, Nova Scotia, Canada.

Pema graduated from the University of California, Berkeley, and worked as an elementary school teacher in California and New Mexico before her conversion to Buddhism.

Following a second divorce, Chödrön began to study with Lama Chime Rinpoche in the French Alps. She became a Buddhist nun in 1974 while studying with him in London. She is a fully ordained bhikṣuṇī in a combination of the Mulasarvastivadin and Dharmaguptaka lineages of vinaya, having received full ordination in Hong Kong in 1981 at the behest of the sixteenth Karmapa. She was probably the first American woman to become fully ordained. She has been instrumental in trying to reestablish full ordination for nuns in the Mulasarvastivadin order, to which all Tibetan Buddhist monastics have traditionally belonged.

Contact for details: http://pemachodronfoundation.org

*   *   *

15. Seeing the emptiness of so much we cling to

Pema Chödrön

Before we can know what natural warmth really is, often we must experience loss. We go along for years moving through our days, propelled by habit, taking life pretty much for granted. Then we or someone dear to us has an accident or gets seriously ill, and it's as if blinders have been removed from our eyes. We see the meaninglessness of so much of what we do and the emptiness of so much we cling to.

When my mother died and I was asked to go through her personal belongings, this awareness hit me hard. She had kept boxes of papers and trinkets that she treasured, things that she held on to through her many moves to smaller and smaller accommodations. They had represented security and comfort for her, and she had been unable to let them go. Now they were just boxes of stuff, things that held no meaning and represented no comfort or security to anyone.

For me these were just empty objects, yet she had clung to them. Seeing this made me sad, and also thoughtful. After that I could never look at my own treasured objects in the same way. I had seen that things themselves are just what they are, neither precious nor worthless, and that all the labels, all our views and opinions about them, are arbitrary.

This was an experience of uncovering basic warmth. The loss of my mother and the pain of seeing so clearly how we impose judgments and values, prejudices, likes and dislikes, onto the world, made me feel great compassion for our shared human predicament. I remember explaining to myself that the whole world consisted of people just like me who were making much ado about nothing and suffering from it tremendously.

Meditation takes us just as we are, with our confusion and our sanity. This complete acceptance of ourselves as we are is a simple, direct relationship with our being. We call this *maitri*, loving-kindness toward ourselves and others. There are four qualities of maitri that are cultivated when we meditate:

1. *Steadfastness*. When we practice meditation we are strengthening our ability to be steadfast with ourselves, in body as well as mind.
2. *Clear seeing*. This is another way of saying that we have less self-deception. Through the process of practicing the technique day in and day out, year after year, we begin to be very honest with ourselves.
3. *Experiencing our emotional distress*. We practice dropping whatever story we are telling ourselves and leaning into the emotions and the fear. We stay with the emotion, experience it, and leave it as it is, without proliferating. Thus we train in opening the fearful heart to the restlessness of our own energy. We learn to abide with the experience of our emotions.
4. *Attention to the present moment*. We make the choice, moment by moment, to be fully here. Attending to our present-moment mind and body is a way of being tender toward self, toward others, and toward the world. This quality of attention is inherent in

our ability to love. These four factors not only apply to sitting meditation, but are essential to all the *bodhichitta* (awakened heart) practices and for relating with difficult situations in our daily lives.

Excerpted from Taking the Leap: Freeing Ourselves From Old Habits and Fears, by Pema Chödrön.

* * *

Geshe Lama Konchog

Geshe Lama Konchog, born Lobsang Puntsog (1917–2001) was a renowned Tibetan Buddhist Gelugpa Lama, who had thousands of followers around the world. Konchog was recognized by the Dalai Lama to be a Great Mahasiddha, or realized guru.

Konchog spent a total of 26 years in isolated mountain retreat, seeking illumination. He studied in Sera Monastery in Tibet from the age of 7 to 32 (1934-1959). Geshe-la had attended initiations and teachings by Pabongka Rinpoche, Trijang Rinpoche and Pari Rinpoche. He also completed many retreats like Rinchug Gyatsa and other short retreats of the deities he had initiation, staying in the labrangs of these Great Lamas. He completed his Geshe studies and was about to take his final exams in 1959, but had to escape Tibet. He left with only the robes he was wearing, a sheepskin and some texts from all four traditions.

Beginning in 1985, he resided at Kopan monastery in Kathmandu, Nepal. He also traveled around the world teaching.

Konchog died at the age of 84 in 2001. His funeral rites, and the search for his subsequent reincarnation (Rinpoche) by his close disciple Tenzin Zopa, are documented in the 2008 film, *Unmistaken Child*.

Contact for details: www.lamayeshe.com

16. Form is empty, emptiness is form: Buddha

Geshe Lama Konchog

There are two categories of beings who should follow the practices of the *Prajnaparamita*—those who are of less intelligence and those of greater intelligence. For those of less intelligence, Avalokiteshvara asked how he should investigate and analyze the profound view of those who hold the lineage of this particular tradition.

Then the noble Avalokiteshvara replied to the venerable Shariputra as follows: "Shariputra, whatever son or daughter of the lineage wishes to engage in the practice of the profound perfection of the wisdom gone beyond, should do it exactly like this. Analyze perfectly and correctly the nature of the five aggregates, which are by nature empty."

This is the short answer. Initially he gave this brief answer, then later on, he elaborated on it by saying: "Form is empty, emptiness is form. Emptiness is no other than form and form is no other than emptiness."

Our physical body is composed of the four elements, the twelve constituents and so forth, and due to the aggregation of all these elements, we are able to label this body "physical".

We are able to say that it is form. However, there is nothing inherently existing in that form from its own side. It is said that the physical form or the form aggregate, lacks inherent existence, but we appear as a physical form. Therefore, the nature of form is equal to the nature of emptiness and emptiness is equal to the nature of form.

These two are considered to be of one nature, yet different in the sense that they are conceptually isolated. This also shows how existence is free from permanence. This is because although the physical form appears, it is empty.

Who posited this physical existence? This physical form was posited by the consciousness. The mind or consciousness posited this physical form, and because the physical form appears to the mind, it therefore lacks inherent, or true, existence.

Due to gaining some understanding of emptiness, we can then eliminate the belief in inherent existence and also by having an understanding of the impermanence of physical form, we can eliminate the thought of eternalism. When we talk about a lack of inherent existence, or say that things do not exist inherently, this itself shows the nominal existence of conventional existence.

From now on the root text describes the practices on the paths of accumulation and preparation. These discussions are based on the fact that we have already generated bodhicitta and we are training in an understanding of emptiness.

The *Heart Sutra* tells us how we should first understand the importance of having a realization of emptiness, and then generate bodhicitta. This is necessary because initially we meditate on the seven instructions of cause and effect to generate bodhicitta. We start to recognize that all sentient beings are our mother and by remembering this kindness, we then want to repay that love, compassion and that extraordinary attitude.

When we generate this extraordinary attitude, the unusual thought of leading all sentient beings to the state of everlasting happiness by ourselves alone is generated. At this time, we then investigate whether it is possible to achieve the state of enlightenment. The reason for doing this is so that we, alone, can lead others out of the state of suffering. But first of all we must be freed from that state ourselves.

Then we investigate whether or not it is possible to be completely freed from all suffering. We need to come to the understanding that when we are able to remove all defilements and delusions from our mental continuum, it is possible to get out of cyclic existence, the state of suffering.

Delusions are caused by the self-grasping attitude. When we realize that we can eliminate this self-grasping attitude, we can get out of the state of suffering.

Excerpted from commentary on The Heart Sutra at lamayeshe. com

*   *   *

Section Five

EVIL, CORRUPTION, SUFFERING

S ri Krishna Prem says it is difficult to understand Lord Krishna's claim that he will always come for the salvation of the good and for the destruction of the wicked. If however we consider the Lilas of Krishna, which are said to be eternal, it is not that Sri Krishna is forever beheading an eternally terrified Kansa in an eternal Mathura, but that the spiritual laws which are symbolized by these acts are always operating in our hearts and in the world, now just as much as five thousand years ago. Now, as then the people are oppressed by evil rulers, but those rulers are not any material kings but desire, anger, greed and delusion.

As J. Krishnamurti's personal chef, Michael Krohnen used to record his conversations at the dining table. On the question of corruption, Krishnamurti once insisted on putting it right on everyone's doorstep, "Put yourself that question: 'why am I corrupt?'" Probing for the inner cause of this pervasive corruption, he tentatively offered any number of answers, which none of us had entertained. "Is it knowledge?" he asked. "Is it the tremendous importance given to the intellect?"

Free will and the suffering arising from separative existence may after all be the design of the Lord, according to Swami Abhayananda. He asks, "The soul's ability to will freely – had He no hand in that? May it not be that our embodied existence in this spatio-temporal world is also His doing? Is it not possible that this going forth into the school of separate existence is, as the Vedantists assert, His play or sport? And is it not possible that we are sent forth into this material school to prove and improve, to be tested and to evolve in His knowledge, in His joy?"

*   *   *

Krishna Prem

Ronald Henry Nixon (1898 – 1965), later known as Krishna Prem was a British spiritual aspirant who went to India in the early 20th century. Together with his spiritual teacher Yashoda Ma, he founded an ashram at Mirtola, near Almora, India. He was one of the first Europeans to pursue orthodox Vaishnavite Hinduism.

At age 18, Nixon became a British fighter pilot in the First World War. On one occasion, he experienced an escape from death that he believed was miraculous, in which a "power beyond our ken" saved him from several enemy planes.

In 1921 Nixon accepted the offer of a teaching position at the University of Lucknow, in northern India. The university's vice chancellor, Gyanendra Nath Chakravarti, was also spiritually inclined and offered Nixon assistance. Over time, Nixon came to regard Gyanendra's wife, Monika Chakravarti, as his spiritual teacher. In 1928, Monika took vows of renunciation in the Gaudiya Vaishnavite tradition and adopted the monastic name of Yashoda Ma. She initiated Nixon into vairagya, and he adopted Krishna Prem as his monastic name.

In 1948 he visited South India, meeting Sri Ramana Maharshi, as well as Sri Aurobindo and Mirra Alfassa ("The Mother"). Ramana Maharshi commended Krishnaprem to his devotees with the words, 'A wonderful blend of gyani (knowledge) and bhakti (devotion) in one person.'

Contact for details: www.yogamag.net

* * *

17. Will Krishna be born again to destroy present evil?

Srikrishna Prem (Ronald Nixon)

All know Sri Krishna's statement that he comes for the salvation of the good and for the destruction of the wicked, but, if this is a mere historical fact, if this destruction of the wicked merely took place at the end of Dwapara Yuga, then it will be but small consolation to those who seek salvation now, or are oppressed by the wicked in this twentieth century. If on the other hand, it is said that He saves the good and destroys the wicked at all times, then it will not be clear what is the necessity of Avatars at all.

In the first place, who are these wicked ones who are destroyed by the Lord? We all like to flatter ourselves that we are the good, and that those who oppose us are the wicked. Did not both parties in the late war pray to God utterly to destroy their wicked enemies and to save their righteous selves? It pleases us to think that all our misfortunes are the result of the wickedness of our oppressors and that, if they were destroyed or converted, we should be perfectly all right. But this is an entire delusion. It is not external enemies who oppress us, but we ourselves who oppress ourselves.

"The self, verily, is the friend of the self; and the self also is the enemy of the self." (Gita.)

He who appears to oppress me from without is but the instrument of my own karma; his destruction would in no way lessen my sufferings. It is my own evil desires and tendencies that are my oppressors; it is they who cause me to suffer; and it is they who are the wicked who must be destroyed.

But how is the fact that an Avatara took place in Dwapara Yuga, or at any other time, going to effect the destruction of the six enemies so firmly established in my heart? In fact it is not going to do so if my idea of an Avatara is merely one of some wondrous Divine hero who descended on this earth long ago, performed His marvelous feats and then vanished once more.

In reality, the actions of an Avatara are all symbolic, and were performed in order to teach desire-blind mortals those inner truths which they are not able to perceive with their own unaided vision. That the Supreme Reality is One, but yet exists in many forms; that all this vast universe exists within that one Reality; that all powers, 'bad' as well as 'good', issue forth from Him and in the end return to Him; that He is the inner Self of al beings; and that no bonds can bind the man who attains to Him; how difficult it is for us to understand these truths.

The mind, used only to dealing with material objects, recoils baffled, and is unable to grasp them in their naked spiritual reality. We may even meditate upon them, but for want of a foothold we can make small progress. If, however, we turn to the contemplation of Sri Krishna's Lilas as related by tradition, our task will become much easier.

We see the one Krishna dancing with the many gopis and each gopi thinking that her Lord is with her alone; we see the whole universe with all of its gods and men within the body of the Lord on Kurukshetra's battlefield; we see the return of Kansa to Krishna, liberated in the very moment of destruction; we see the Divine Charioteer guiding all but bearing no weapons in the great battle, and we see fetters and bolts open of themselves as Vasudeva emerges from the prison with the Divine Child in his arms.

Mediating with love and devotion on the thought of these Lilas, the knowledge of their inner meaning will naturally and automatically spring up in our hearts, and those truths that we failed to understand when presented in the dry form of philosophic statements will come to life in our souls in their essential spiritual nature beyond the range of words or thought.

It is for this reason that the Lilas of Krishna are said to be nitya (eternal). It is not that Sri Krishna is forever beheading an eternally terrified Kansa in an eternal Muttra (Mathura), but that the spiritual laws which are symbolized for our benefit by these acts are always operating in our hearts and in the world, now just as much as five thousand years ago.

Now, as then the people are oppressed by evil rulers, but those rulers are not any material kings. It is kama (desire), krodha (anger), lobha (greed) and moha (delusion), who are the true rulers of this world; our so-called kings are merely puppets in their hands. It is they who oppress us with their tyranny and shut us up in the prison of the body. There, in the darkness of our hearts, the birth of Sri Krishna has to take place or else there can be no salvation for us.

Excerpted from the essay 'The Birth of Sri Krishna' in the 1938 book 'The Search for Truth' published by Book Land, Calcutta

*   *   *

Michael Krohnen

Michael Krohnen was born in Germany and immigrated to the US at age twenty. After attending college in Orange County and San Francisco, he traveled extensively in Europe, Asia and the Americas. During this time he discovered J. Krishnamurti and his teaching and found it singularly enlightening. After attending Krishnamurti's talks on three continents, he joined the Oak Grove School in 1975 as chef de cuisine.

Subsequently he became Krishnamurti's personal chef during K's annual sojourn in California. This unique and profound experience he describes in his book "The Kitchen Chronicles—1001 Lunches with J. Krishnamurti". Currently

Michael Krohnen is the librarian at the Krishnamurti Library, located at the Krishnamurti Education Center.

Krohnen never expected to be a chef. He was a poet, world wanderer and self-described "full-time seeker" until he came across the writings of Krishnamurti in the 1960s. While he was teaching English in Japan, Krohnen heard there was work in California, where a Krishnamurti school was being established.

The openings were for a gardener, maintenance man and cook. Krohnen expected to become the gardener. Instead, he was assigned to cook. "I was deeply shocked at first. It came as a real surprise," he says.

Contact for details: www.kfa.org

18. Investigating the root of corruption

Michael Krohnen

After an interval of silent deliberation, he (J. Krishnamurti) asked simply, "What is corruption?"

After a brief semantic examination, which revealed that 'corruption' meant 'fragmented, broken up', we looked at possible historical causes for the pervasive corruption of human society.

Krishnamurti hesitated to allow the concept of 'society' into the dialogue, since it suggested an entity that was separate, externalized, and both autonomous and anonymous. Invariably, it negated the responsibility of each single human being.

"Society is put together by human beings, it is what we are," he insisted. "Society is not different from us. We are society."

He, thus, firmly anchored the essence and relevance of our discussion. For him, there was nothing theoretical about it. To drive home the point to each one of us present, he altered the phrasing of the question into a simple, direct, "Why am I corrupt?"

He asked the question for us – he clearly felt that he was not corrupt. Nor had I ever witnessed any indication that he might share that common and destructive quality with the rest of us. This inescapably confronted us with the question, as in a mirror. He repeated it intermittently, and the relentless force of self-inquiry inherent in this simple formulation pushed everyone against the wall. Any answer we came up with was swept aside as rationalization and roundabout excuse.

David suggested that people had lost faith in the integrity of society. Someone else cited overpopulation and the concomitant pressure for survival, the search for security, and competition. But Krishnamurti again and again returned to the original question, dissatisfied with any explanation. Vicariously he asked, "Why have I become like this? Why am I corrupt? What has made me corrupt?"

I could observe within myself that one really shied away from seriously putting this question to oneself. Probably not many of those at the table, including myself, really perceived the fact of their corruption. David saw what Krishnamurti was driving at and rephrased the question in an objective form, true to the scientific method, "How does corruption affect the brain?"

Krishnamurti however insisted on putting it right on everyone's doorstep, "Put yourself that question: 'why am I corrupt?'"

Probing for the inner cause of this pervasive corruption, he tentatively offered any number of answers, which none of us had entertained.

"Is it knowledge?" he asked. "Is it the tremendous importance given to the intellect?"

He never seemed quite ready to accept an answer, even his own. He remained in a state of not-knowing; he kept on probing, pushing, questioning, never allowing any formulation, however plausible, to become a conclusion. A conclusion was a dead end for him. Finally, after repeating the question, "Why am I corrupt?" between twenty and thirty times over a two-hour period, he made that enormous quantum leap that only he seemed capable of.

It was the unthought-of, inconceivable *dénouement* of a spellbinding psychological thriller, in which we were all participants, victims, perpetrators. And the 180-degree turn from the horizontal to the vertical plane, imbued with clarity and simplicity, was something none of us had envisioned.

Even so, he refrained from insisting that his proposition was right. The beauty of the argument dwelt in questioning the question, or rather the motive behind it. He suggested that wanting a conclusion – which essentially implied knowing the cause, which then in turn would become knowledge – was itself corruption. Wanting to find the cause of a problem was the same thing. That which had been causing corruption, that is, thought and knowledge, were also asking the question.

Was this a case of leading the argument *ad absurdum*?, I asked myself. Or was it the beauty of an investigation into *what is* – a movement from nothingness into nothingness? To positively clarify the point he was making – and I think he fully meant what he said at that moment – Krishnamurti simply stated, "I don't want to know."

Who could keep pace with that?

Excerpted from: Michael Krohnen – 'The Kitchen Chronicles: 1001 Lunches with J. Krishnamurti', pages 216 – 218; Edwin House Publishing, Ojai, California 1997, published in India by Penguin India, 1997

*   *   *

Swami Abhayananda

Swami Abhayananda was born Stan Trout (1938) in Indianapolis. He experienced a 'spiritual awakening' at the age of 28 and subsequently went on a retreat for five years, in the Santa Cruz mountains of California. In 1972 he went to India and studied under Swami Muktananda for two years, after which he returned to the USA and lived and served in his ashrams there, taking on many responsibilities as a monk.

In 1981 he became disillusioned with Muktananda (discovering the latter had been abusing his position) and left the organization. Continued his studies, writing and teaching. Now lives in Florida.

In his own words, on his website, he says, "I am not hindered by organizational ties or religious affiliation, and so my vision and my philosophy is my own, and not restricted to the mystical tradition of either the East or the West. Today, I live a simple, solitary life, devoted to meditation on God and the sharing of His truth."

He is the author of the classic *History of Mysticism*, *The Wisdom of Vedanta* and *The Supreme Self.*

Contact for details: *http://themysticsvision.weebly.com*

* * *

19. Suffering due to separative will of the individual

Swami Abhayananda (Stan Trout)

There is one spiritual issue on which science, secular society, and the various religious traditions all agree: the freedom and accountability of the human will. The ancient Jews were keenly aware of the fact that it was man's free will that allowed for the disobedience of God's will, as illustrated in their Biblical 'Garden of Eden' story.

Later, Christians declared that God sacrificed His own son on the cross to redeem 'believers' from that earlier 'Fall from grace'. Other spiritual teachers, such as the Buddha, Shankara and Plotinus, also postulate the human 'will to separateness' as the instigator of human suffering. Here, for example, is Plotinus' take on man's Fall:

"What can it be that has brought the souls to forget the Father, God, and, though [they are] members of the Divine and entirely of that world, to ignore at once themselves and It? The evil that has overtaken them has its source in self-will, in the entry into the sphere of process, and in the primal differentiation with the desire for self-ownership. They conceived a pleasure in this freedom and largely indulged their own motion. Thus they were hurried down the wrong path, and in the end, drifting further and further, they came to lose even the thought of their origin in the Divine."

The Jews, Christians, the Buddha, Shankara, Plotinus – all put the blame for human suffering upon the separative will of the individual. And rightly so, no doubt; for in the Divine Itself, there is no suffering. Had the One no hand, then, in the creation of the defiant soul? Must we not wonder if anything at all comes to pass that is not of His doing?

The soul's ability to will freely – had He no hand in that? May it not be that our embodied existence in this spatio-temporal world is also His doing? Is it not possible that this going forth into the school of separate existence is, as the Vedantists assert, His play or sport? And is it not possible that we are sent forth into this material school to prove and improve, to be tested and to evolve in His knowledge, in His joy?

It is indeed we who create suffering through ignorance and error; but it is He who comprises the essence of this soul with its capacity for willing, and it is He who fashioned this universal school for the soul's correcting. Can we imagine that He was ignorant of the outcome?

We are but waves on His infinite ocean; and while the wave's suffering of separation from the ocean might seem real enough to the wave, it is actually based on illusion. Once the wave realizes its true nature, all suffering disappears.

We are in a similar situation: unknowing, we suffer; knowing, we rejoice. It is not existence that constitutes suffering, but existence in delusion. When we awake to our Divine existence, all suffering vanishes. Is this not the message of all who have seen the truth?

All creatures, down to the smallest microbes, and up to the great apes, have the power of will; but only the creature known as man has the ability to know his Source and Ground as Spirit, and strive to overcome his merely fleshly impulses. Is that circumstance only accidental, or is there a purposeful evolution at work here?

Man is the culmination of God's purposes; and only he is able to find within himself the eternal One. It's true that, in following his own appetites and cravings, man brings himself to know suffering; but, even though the expanse presented before him is broad and vast and his opportunities many, experience leads him inexorably to wisdom; the Divine in him leads him eventually to Itself.

Excerpted from the essay 'How God Made the World' encapsulating ideas expressed in the book 'Body and Soul' http://themysticsvision.weebly.com

*   *   *

Section Six

GOD, DIVINE

Meister Eckhart counsels us to keep silent and not continue talking about God. According to him, "whenever you prate about God, you lie, and commit sin. If you will be without sin, prate not about God. You can understand nothing about God, for He is above all understanding. Eckhart feels that if you really love God, nothing would give you greater pleasure than abiding in His Will.

Seeking to know her view, a student present in the audience told Jillellamudi Amma that he thought Buddha was greater than either Rama or Krishna. After a pragmatic silence of a few minutes Amma said: 'In my view you are as great as either Rama or Krishna or Buddha.' Those present thought that Amma was making fun of the questioner. But she was not. She continued; 'Rama came with a purpose. He has completed and he left. So did Krishna or Buddha. They played their allotted roles. So will you. I find no difference.'

Tarun Sardana writes about a seeker called Vivek who is asked by his Guru to close his eyes and describe what he sees. Vivek closes his eyes but sees only darkness. He asks for the Guru's grace to be able to go in. The Guru says his grace is available but it is very important that he makes the discovery on his own. "Don't get hassled. Dive deep within and you'll find it." So this time Vivek goes much deeper.

William Wildblood speaks out against the distorted version of non-duality now prevalent. You can't transcend duality by denying it, rejecting it or pretending that it is not there. You must fully acknowledge it and all it implies, and then go beyond it. He quotes the Masters' profound saying 'Remember the Creator,' and points out that this is something non-dualists of the modern Western variety frequently fail to do.

Anandamayi Ma advises that when reading, we should read about God, when talking, talk of God and when singing, sing His praises. These three practices are intrinsically the same, she says, but because people respond differently, the same is expressed in three different ways to suit each person's temperament and capacity for assimilation. Essentially there is only He and He alone, although everyone has his own individual path that leads to Him.

* * *

Meister Eckhart

Eckhart von Hochheim (1260–1327), commonly known as Meister Eckhart, was a German theologian, philosopher and mystic, born near Gotha, in the Landgraviate of Thuringia in the Holy Roman Empire.

Eckhart came into prominence during the Avignon Papacy, at a time of increased tensions between the Franciscan Order and Eckhart's Dominican Order of

Preachers. In later life he was accused of heresy and brought up before the local Franciscan-led Inquisition, and tried as a heretic by Pope John XXII. He probably died before his verdict was received.

He was well known for his work with pious lay groups such as the Friends of God. Within popular spirituality he has acquired a status as a great mystic.

Contact for details: sermonindex.net

* * *

20. Whatever God gives or gives not, is the best

Meister Eckhart

You should know, that that which God gives to those men who seek to do His will with all their might, is the best. Of this thou mayest be as sure, as thou art sure that God lives, that the very best must necessarily be, and that in no other way could anything better happen. Even if something else seems better, it would not be so good for thee, for God wills this and not another way, and this way must be the best for thee.

Whether it be sickness or poverty or hunger or thirst, or whatever it be, that God hangs over thee or does not hang over thee – whatever God gives or gives not, that is all what is best for thee; whether it be devotion or inwardness, or the lack of these which grieves thee – only set thyself right in this, that thou desirest the glory of God in all things, and then whatever He does to thee, that is the best.

Now thou mayest perchance say: How can I tell whether it is the will of God or not? If it were not the will of God, it would not happen. Thou couldst have neither sickness nor anything else unless God willed it. But know that it is God's will that thou shouldst have so much pleasure and satisfaction therein, that thou shouldst feel no pain as pain; thou shouldst take it from God as the very best thing, for it must of necessity be the very best thing for thee. Therefore I may even wish for it and desire it, and nothing would become me better than so to do.

God is nameless, for no man can either say or understand aught about Him. If I say, God is good, it is not true; nay more; I am good, God is not good. I may even say, I am better than God; for whatever is good, may become better, and whatever may become better, may become best. Now God is not good, for He cannot become better. And if He cannot become better, He cannot become best, for these three things, good, better, and best, are far from God, since He is above all.

If I also say, God is wise, it is not true; I am wiser than He. If I also say, God is a Being, it is not true; He is transcendent Being and superessential Nothingness. Concerning this St Augustine says: the best thing that man can say about God is to be able to be silent about Him, from the wisdom of his inner judgment.

Therefore be silent and prate not about God, for whenever thou dost prate about God, thou liest, and committest sin. If thou wilt be without sin, prate not about God. Thou canst understand nought about God, for He is above all understanding. A master saith: If I had a God whom I could understand, I would never hold Him to be God.

If you loved God, of a surety nothing would give you greater pleasure than what pleases Him best, and that whereby His will may be most fully done.

Excerpted from sermonindex.net

* * *

Jillellamudi Amma

Jillellamudi Amma or Anasuya Devi (1923-1985) was born at Mannava, a small village in Guntur District of Andhra Pradesh, India.

She used to have long trances even as a child. As a little girl, she never asked for food just as she never cried for milk as an infant. She accepted food if it was given, only to give to somebody else who was in need of it. In later life, Amma would frequently go for long periods without eating, even abandoning all liquids usually considered as essential for survival.

It was a curious paradox of Amma's life that being indifferent to eating herself, she spent a large portion of her time and energy in feeding others. Once Amma commented humorously "You grow weak if you don't eat, but I grow weak if I don't feed".

In 1936, Amma married Brahmandam Nageswara Rao. When a disciple asked her why she needs to get married, she told him that it was only to show that marriage need not be feared as an obstacle to one's spiritual progress. Amma was often persecuted and harassed by the ignorant and jealous villagers.

Amma saw only good in people and had no concept of "Sin" whatsoever. In many cases, people's chronic psychological problems, physical diseases, financial difficulties, bad habits, addictions and negative attitudes (pride, envy, shame, pettiness and so on) would be cleared by the simple look or utterance from Amma. Amma gave no discourses, but responded to people's questions regarding divine truth with short utterances full of meaning.

Contact for details: *www.motherofall.org*

* * *

21. 'You are as great as Rama, Krishna or Buddha'

Jillellamudi Amma

Questioner: Are God and the human soul different, or is man himself God? Is it true that the maturity of the human mind is Divinity?

Amma: If you ask, "what is true and what is false?" I say all that appears is true. We are using the name 'God'. For whom? For what kind of a being? We don't know what He is like. We don't know the meaning of that word 'God'. 'God' means 'what is', 'Truth, Reality. What is Reality? 'What is', 'what is', is God.

In answer to your question, I say that man, you, I – all that appears is God. We hear it said that God is formless and invisible. 'God' means 'Reality'. What is Reality? All that is seen as objects – water, air, fire light – isn't this Reality?

They say, "For these objects to have come into being, and for these to have become so many, there must have been some cause." Did the forms come through God, or are the forms themselves God? All that appears is God. I have not seen a form that differs and is separate from all this which appears. Creation is God. There is nothing other than this entire creation. Creation is that which has become many.

I am just like you

I have all the same qualities which you have. I am just like you. They worship me because, owing to their purity of heart, they see the divine in me. But I am in no way different from you. I experience pain and pleasure, attachment and bereavement just as you do. The only difference is that I don't try to shun pain and sorrow. I abandon myself to them without the least inhibition.

Richard Schiffman, writing in his book 'Mother of All' describes the atmosphere of visiting Jillellamudi thus: Those were good old days, when there was no road to Jillellamudi, no buildings, no telephones, no water supply, no electricity and blurring of loud speakers. One had to walk from the 7th mile with his load on his back or head. Many a time, one had to wade thru knee deep or even neck deep waters with all the attending perils of unseen thrones, rocks, pits and reptiles.

"But at the end of all that, the presence of Amma more than compensated all his toils. Only a staunch and determined few braved all these trials and tribulations and enjoyed unforgettable moments of bliss in the proximity of Amma, and Amma alone. Unlike now, there were no disturbing and distracting things or thoughts.

"On one such beautiful clear moonlight night in 1959, a few brothers and sisters clustered around Amma, seated on a low uncomfortable cot and narrating stories in such a humorous way that everyone rolled with mirth.

"Among those present was a student of Hindu College, Guntur, who expressed an opinion: 'Amma! In my view Buddha is greater than either Rama or Krishna? What do you say?' After a pragmatic silence of a few minutes Amma said: 'In my view you are as great as either Rama or Krishna or Buddha.'

Those present thought that Amma was making fun of the questioner. But she was not. She continued; 'Rama came with a purpose. He has completed and he left. So did Krishna or Buddha. They played their allotted roles. So will you. I find no difference.'

A hush fell on the audience. For a while no one spoke, moved or breathed. They were all trying to bridge the wide conceptual gap, each in his own way.

"A word of caution. This is not to equate those incarnations with mere mortals. It is just to highlight the dizzy height at which Amma stands from where all the hills and dales look alike."

Excerpted from http://www.motherofall.org

*   *   *

Tarun Sardana

Tarun Sardana (born 1979) stays in Delhi, India with his parents, wife and little son. He worked as a software professional both in India and abroad. He quit his successful corporate career as a project manager with a fortune 500 company to devote the rest of his time in knowing the "I".

His grandmom and mom are spiritual followers and used to read sacred scriptures and share with him and his younger brother their spiritual experiences. In school, he was taught the history of Sikhism as part of curriculum as it was a Sikh school. He always wanted to understand what is 'that' which every scripture points at.

He used to lock himself for hours in a room meditating and seeking that truth, seeking God until one day when he came across one of Ramana Maharishi's articles on web which changed his direction of search from finding God to finding the one who is seeking God.

Tarun is also an author of the book titled 'Dissolved', which is based on 'Advaita' (non duality). It was released in October 2009 and has already gained popularity amongst the non-duality followers both in India and abroad.

Contact for details: www.knowi.org

* * *

22. A state where the seeker dissolves in the Self

Tarun Sardana

The journey to the Self is a little complicated: The more one walks towards it, the farther it goes; the moment one stops, one finds oneself there. "Dissolved" is a state where two become one. Just as a river dissolves in the ocean, a raindrop in the water, a fragrance in the air, and a seeker in the Self.

The book "Dissolved "is about the journey of a seeker, Vivek, who goes within to seek the truth and in the process becomes one with it. This is a parable of the dissolving of the ego-self in the ocean of blissful, all pervading Self – the only Truth. The following is an excerpt from the book:

Guru Ji: Listen Vivek. Now I will share with you the highest of all wisdom. I would like you to close your eyes and tell me, what do you see?

Vivek: (Bows down to Guru Ji and closes his eyes. After a while, he speaks up) I see nothing Guru Ji. It is all blank. Nothing in there.
(Vivek opens his eyes)

Guru Ji: We are not done yet, Son. Keep your eyes closed.
(Vivek apologizes, bows down to Guru Ji and closes his eyes again)

Guru Ji: So what do you see?

Vivek: There is nothing in there Guru Ji. It's all dark. It's all empty.

Guru Ji: If your eyes are closed, who is the one, who sees this darkness?
(Long silence. Vivek breaks the silence and speaks up)

Vivek: I don't know Guru Ji. I mean, it is me but I can't see myself.

Guru Ji: Dont worry, Vivek. Just take some more time and see who is this "ME", who sees this darkness.
(Long silence. No movement. Complete, perfect silence. Vivek has lost track of time. Everything has come to a standstill. Vivek again breaks the silence and speaks up)

Vivek: Please help me Guru Ji. I am not able to see myself. I have been doing everything for me up till now but I am not able to see myself. Please be kind and tell me: Who am I?

Guru Ji: I can understand your dilemma Vivek, but it is very important that you find it on your own. My grace is with you, so don't be scared. Go deep within. Your true Self is already waiting to uncover itself. It has been waiting for years. So don't get hassled. Dive deep within and you'll find it.

This time the Silence is much longer. There is no movement. It appears as if Vivek has left his body. Hours pass . . . Days pass . . . Still no movement . . . Outside, there is complete silence. Inside, whatever was happening only Guru Ji knew or Vivek, if there was still any Vivek left.

Scriptures say, to realize the ultimate truth one has to die. Is this the death, they talk about? Vivek was dead for the outside world. Rain, storms, days, nights, hunger . . . had no effect on him. His breath had stopped.

After a long interval, Vivek opened his eyes, looked at Guru Ji, smiled and bowed before him. This time, he had no questions. His eyes were steady and calm. His face reflected peace. He had nothing but silence to share with Guru Ji.

Excerpted from 'Dissolved'

*   *   *

William Wildblood

William Wildblood was born in London in 1955, and educated at Westminster School. After a period working as an antiques dealer, he left the U.K. He ran a guesthouse in South India for several years and then another in France where he was also an occasional guide at the medieval abbey of le Mont Saint-Michel.

He returned to England at the end of the 20th century since when he has worked for BBC magazines in various capacities, including seven years as an antiques columnist.

His book *Meeting the Masters,* which describes his experiences with a group of discarnate spiritual beings and the training he was given by them, was published in 2012, and he has a blog which further develops themes from the book.

Contact for details: http://meetingthemasters.blogspot.co.uk.

23. Spirituality without recognition of a higher power is a trap

William Wildblood

There was a time when I would unreservedly have described myself as a partisan of non-duality. Today I regard it as potentially one of the more misleading forms of spirituality though I still believe it describes the basic truth of the universe. What has changed in my outlook?

What has changed is the fact that so many people now embrace (or even teach) non-duality in a form that would not have been recognized by its originators in India (Note: non-duality is found in many places but I take the Indian version as the principal source of the doctrine).

So it is not non-duality that is the problem. That remains as pure truth. It is the distorted version of those who think themselves in the vanguard of spirituality but who dispense with God because of what can only be called lack of humility and intellectual arrogance. What these people don't appreciate is that you should come to non-duality as the basis of your approach to God and the universe only after having fully traversed duality. For duality is real. It may not be the ultimate reality but ultimate reality comes only at the end.

Non-duality is a step beyond duality but that does not mean that it completely replaces it. Non-duality says that all is one. The division between spirit and matter is false, and you are pure undivided consciousness. All this is absolutely true, and actually pretty easy to understand as a concept and even to attain as an experience in meditation or, at least, to imagine one has attained.

However what is equally true is that the duality of the soul and its Creator is a real one, even if it must eventually be transcended. But, and this is what is at issue, you won't transcend it by denying it, rejecting it or pretending that it is not there. You must fully acknowledge it and all it implies, and then go beyond it.

That's the only way, and those who are encouraged to bypass the traditional approach, which is founded on wisdom and insight, by teachers of half-truths who lack these things, even if they have an intellectual grasp of that of which they teach, are being misled.

Worse, they are being sidetracked from the true path and their spiritual development delayed.

You are pure awareness

Such a simple statement to make, but how do you transcend the duality of subject and object and know yourself to be pure awareness? Not just by thinking so, that's certain. And is pure awareness all you are? Because if not then maybe it's not sufficient to take that, and that alone, as the basis of your spiritual practice. One of the Masters' simplest but most profound sayings was 'Remember the Creator'.

This is something non-dualists of the modern Western variety frequently fail to do. Usually brought up in one of the monotheistic religions, or a society still heavily influenced by that, they are eager to throw off their cultural baggage, which they perceive as outworn (and I am not saying that it is not in many ways), but they still crave some form of spirituality.

A non-dualistic belief system fits the bill because, in its trivialized version, it makes relatively few demands of the lower self, and does not require one to bend the knee or incline the head. But spirituality without a recognition of a higher power is a temptation to be avoided, though very attractive to the ego that always wants to reap the benefits of spirituality without giving itself up.

The true non-dualist always remembers the Creator (though he may not phrase it exactly like that) because he knows that he is part of God. For the false non-dualist it is the other way around. He is pure consciousness.

Excerpted from http://meetingthemasters.blogspot.co.uk

*   *   *

Anandamayi Ma

Anandamayi Ma (1896-1981) was born in East Bengal (now Bangladesh). She was very sensitive to religious ritual as a child, and the sound of religious chanting would bring about ecstatic feelings in her. She was married at 13 to Ramani Mohan Cakravarti or Bholanath. It was a celibate marriage though not by her husband's choice. When thoughts of sexuality occurred to Bholanath, Anandamayi's body would take on the qualities of death. Later, Bholanath took initiation from her and accepted Anandamayi as his guru.

Inner voices would tell her what actions to perform. She would shed profuse tears, laugh for hours, and talk at tremendous speed in a Sanskrit-like language. She would also fast for long periods and at other times consume enough food for eight or nine people.

Anandamayi traveled throughout India. She was known for her yogic powers where she could read her devotee's thoughts and emotions at a distance, make her body shrink and expand, and cure the sick.

She claimed that all the outer changes in her life were for the benefit of her disciples. She influenced the spirituality of thousands of people who came to see her throughout her life.

Contact for details: www.anandamayi.org

*   *   *

24. God must be the alpha and omega of whatever is done

Anandamayi Ma

Be it the perusal of Sacred Texts, listening to religious discourses, engaging in kirtan – God must be the alpha and omega of whatever is done. When reading, read about Him, when talking, talk of Him and when singing, sing His praises. These three practices are intrinsically the same; but because people respond differently, the same is expressed in three different ways to suit each person's temperament and capacity for assimilation.

Essentially there is only He and He alone, although everyone has his own individual path that leads to Him. What is the right path for each, depends on his personal predilection, based on the specific character of his inner qualifications.

First comes listening, then reflection, and last of all the translation into action of what has been heard and pondered over. This is why one has first of all to listen, so that later on each may be able to select Vedanta or kirtan or whatever else be in his own line.

Have you never come across people making light of kirtan, saying: "What is there to be gained by it?" Nevertheless, after listening to it for some length of time, they actually develop a liking for it. Therefore one must listen before one can reflect, and then later, what has been heard and reflected upon will take shape in action suited to the person concerned.

To listen to discourses on God or Truth is certainly beneficial, provided one does not allow oneself to be moved by a spirit of fault-finding or disparagement, should there be differences of outlook to one's own. To find fault with others creates obstacles for everyone all around: for him who criticizes, for him who is blamed, as well as for those who listen to the criticism. Whereas, what is said in a spirit of appreciation is fruitful to everybody.

For only where there is no question of regarding anything as inferior or blameworthy (asat) can one call it Satsang – a play upon words: Sat means True Being, the Good; satsang the company of the good, and also a religious gathering. Asat, the opposite of sat, means non-being, wrong, evil.

Therefore to find fault (asat) in a religious meeting (satsang) is a contradiction in terms.

Question: When will there be peace on earth?

Sri Ma: Well, you know what the present state of affairs is; things are happening as they are destined to be.

Q: When will this state of unrest come to an end?

Sri Ma: The fact that many of you feel concerned about it and ask: 'When will it end?' is also one of the ways of His Self-manifestation.

Jagat (world) means ceaseless movement, and obviously there can be no rest in movement. How could there be peace in perpetual coming and going? Peace reigns where no coming exists and no going, no melting and no burning. Reverse your course, advance towards Him then there will be hope of peace.

By your japa and meditation those who are close to you will also benefit through the helpful influence of your presence. In order to develop a taste for meditation you have to make a deliberate and sustained effort, just as children have to be made to sit and study, be it by persuasion or coercion. Even if you do not feel inclined to meditate, conquer your reluctance and make an attempt.

The habit of countless lives is pulling you in the opposite direction and making it difficult for you – persevere in spite of it!

Some severe blow of fate will drive you towards God. This will be but an expression of His Mercy; however painful, it is by such blows that one learns one's lesson.

Excerpted from 'Words of Sri Anandamayi Ma,' translated and compiled by Atmananda. www.anandamayi.org

* * *

Section Seven

GURU, MOTHER

S wami Sivananda says a Guru is absolutely necessary for every aspirant on the spiritual path. "The nature of egoism is such that you will not be able to find out your own defects. Just as a man cannot see his back, so also he cannot see his own errors. He must live under a Guru for the eradication of his evil qualities and defects." It is tough to find your way on the spiritual path. "The mind will mislead you very often. The Guru will be able to remove pitfalls and obstacles, and lead you along the right path."

A meeting took place between J. Krishnamurti and Anandamayee Ma in the Delhi where the latter asked him why he spoke so much against Gurus? "When you say one does not need any Guru, sadhana etc., you automatically become the Guru of those who accept your view." Krishnamurti put forward his view that if you discuss your problems with a friend he does not thereby become your Guru etc. "If a dog barks in the dark and alerts you to a snake, the dog does not thereby become your Guru!"

A devotee asked Sri Ramakrishna if the Mother so wanted, would she not give freedom to all? Then why has She kept us bound to the world? The Master replied: "That is Her will. She wants to continue playing with Her created beings. In a game of hide-and-seek the running about soon stops if in the beginning all the players touch the 'granny'. If all touch her, then how can the game go on? That displeases her. Her pleasure is in continuing the game. It is as if the Divine Mother said to the human mind in confidence, with a sign from Her eye, 'Go and enjoy the world.'

*   *   *

Swami Sivananda

Swami Sivananda (1887 – 1963) was a Hindu spiritual teacher and a proponent of Yoga and Vedanta. Born as Kuppuswami in Pattamadai, in the Tirunelveli district of Tamil Nadu, India, he studied medicine and served in British Malaya as a physician for 10 years. When he was 35, his wife and one child died. At that point he dropped everything and set off, sleeping on the road, begging from door to door, from Singapore to Himalayas.

He travelled all around India and visited important pilgrimage places from the south, including Rameswaram. He reached Sri Aurobindo ashram and met Suddhananda Bharati Maharishi. In the Ramana ashram, he had the vision (darshan) of Ramana Maharishi, on the latter's birthday. He sang Bhajanas and danced until he reached ecstasy, along with Ramana bhaktas.

In 1924, he met his Guru Vishwānanda Saraswati in Rishikesh who initiated him into the Sannyasa order. Sivānanda performed austerities for many years but he also continued to nurse the sick. He was the founder of The

Divine Life Society (1936), Yoga-Vedanta Forest Academy
(1948) and author of over 200 books on yoga, Vedanta and
a variety of subjects.

Contact for details: www.sivananda.org

25. Guru protects you from being led astray

Swami Sivananda

For a beginner in the spiritual path, a Guru is necessary.
To light a candle, you need a burning candle. Even an
illumined soul alone can enlighten another soul.

Some do meditation for some years independently.
Later, they actually feel the necessity of a Guru. They come
across some obstacles in the way.

They are unable to know how to obviate these
impediments or stumbling blocks. Then they begin to
search for a Master.

Only the man who has already been to Badrinath will
be able to tell you the road. In the case of the spiritual path,
it is still more difficult to find your way. The mind will
mislead you very often. The Guru will be able to remove
pitfalls and obstacles, and lead you along the right path. He
will tell you:

"This road leads you to Moksha (liberation); this one
leads to bondage".

Without this guidance, you might want to go to
Badrinath, but find yourself in Delhi!

The scriptures are like a forest. There are ambiguous
passages. There are passages which are apparently

contradictory. There are passages which have esoteric meanings, diverse significance, and hidden explanations.

There are cross-references. You are in need of a Guru or Preceptor who will explain to you the right meaning, who will remove doubts and ambiguities, who will place before you the essence of the teachings.

A Guru is absolutely necessary for every aspirant in the spiritual path. It is only the Guru who will find out your defects. The nature of egoism is such that you will not be able to find out your own defects. Just as a man cannot see his back, so also he cannot see his own errors. He must live under a Guru for the eradication of his evil qualities and defects.

The aspirant who is under the guidance of a Master or Guru is safe from being led astray. Satsanga or association with the Guru is an amour and fortress to guard you against all temptations and unfavorable forces of the material world.

Cases of those who had attained perfection without study under any Guru should not be cited as authority against the necessity of a Guru; for, such great men are the anomalies of spiritual life, and not the common normality.

They come into existence as spiritual masters as a result of the intense service, study, and meditation practiced in previous births.

They had already studied under the Guru. The present birth is only its continuative spiritual effect. Hence, the importance of the Guru is not lessened thereby.

Some teachers mislead their aspirants. They say unto all: "Think for yourself. Do not surrender yourself to any Guru". When one says, "Do not follow any Guru!", he intends to be the listeners' Guru himself. Do not approach such pseudo-Gurus. Do not hear their lectures.

All great ones had their teachers. All the sages, saints, prophets, world teachers, incarnations, great men, have had their own Gurus, however great they might have been. Svetaketu learnt the nature of Truth from Uddalaka, Maitreyi from Yajnavalkya, Bhrigu from Varuna, Narada from Sanatkumara, Nachiketas from Yama, Indra from Prajapati; and several others humbly went to wise ones, observed strict Brahmacharya, practiced rigorous discipline, and learnt Brahma-vidya (the science of God) from them.

Lord Krishna sat at the feet of His Guru Sandeepani. Lord Rama had Guru Vasishtha who gave Him Upadesha (spiritual advice). Lord Jesus sought John to be baptized by him on the banks of the river Jordan. Even Devas (celestial beings) have Brihaspati as their Guru. Even the greatest among the divine beings sat at the feet of Guru Dakshinamurti.

A neophyte must have a personal Guru first. He cannot have God as Guru to begin with.

Excerpted from Guru Tattwa by Swami Sivananda http://www.dlshq.org

*   *   *

Atmananda (Blanca)

Blanca, (1904-1985) a former Austrian aristocrat, became a renunciate under Anandmayi Ma, receiving from Ma the name "Atmananda". She performed for Westerners an invaluable service by translating Ma's teachings into English and other European languages.

Blanca originally came to India because of Jiddu Krishnamurti. Already as a teenager she was taken in by him, and finally taught English for full 18 years in his school in Varanasi. And by the side she gave piano concerts for All India Radio.

Later, she was fascinated by Anandamayi Ma and became her disciple. In her she found what she had been searching for. She felt she was saved.

'Death Must Die' compiled and edited by **Ram Alexander**, is based on the diaries of Atmananda. It gives an intimate first-hand account of a courageous woman's spiritual quest in close association with several of India's greatest modern saints. Ram Alexander, who was a close friend of Atmananda's and a fellow disciple of Anandamayi Ma, writes with insight about the guru-disciple relationship.

Contact for details: www.anandamayi.org

* * *

26. J. Krishnamurti & Anandamayi Ma discuss the Guru

Atmananda (Blanca of Vienna)

Mother (Anandamayi Ma) met J.Krishnamurti in Delhi. He was staying at Kitty's house and the meeting took place in her garden. Mother told us all about it (in Bengali). She related how She told J.K.: "Pitaji, why do you speak against Gurus? When you say one does not need any Guru, sadhana etc., you automatically become the Guru of those who accept your view, particularly as large numbers of people come to hear you speak and are influenced by you."

He: "No, if you discuss your problems with a friend he does not thereby become your Guru etc. If a dog barks in the dark and alerts you to a snake, the dog does not thereby become your Guru!" At the end he took Her hand in both his and said: "I hope to meet you again soon".

She commented: "Paramananda and others say that he [J.K.] has one 'dosh'[fault]: While his way is certainly valid he does not accept the validity of approaches other than his own —which is one of vichara [self-inquiry]."

I feel very happy that She met him, it seems to make everything so much easier for me. I need not explain anything to Her."

In her authoritative biography of J. Krishnamurti, Pupul Jayakar describes the meeting between Krishnamurti and Anandamayee which took place in the Delhi home of Kitty Shiva Rao. "They met in the garden, as the mother never entered the home of a householder. She did not speak English, and spoke through a translator (Krishnamurti no longer spoke any Indian language). She had a radiant smiling presence. She said that she had seen a photograph of Krishnamurti many years before and knew that he was very great".

A description of the conversation already narrated by Atmananda follows with the difference that Anandamayee Ma has the last word, gently insisting that in the act of setting himself up as a public spiritual authority, he cannot avoid the responsibility of being a Guru, the very thing he rails against. After this: "He held her hand gently and did not answer."

Pupul Jayakar continues: "Many visitors came and prostrated themselves at the feet of K. and Anandamayee Ma. Anandamayee Ma accepted their greetings, but Krishnaji was embarrassed. As always he would not permit them to bow down but sprang to his feet and bent down to touch the feet of the seeker of blessing. Later after Anandamayee left, Krishnaji spoke of her with warmth and affection. There had been communication, though much of it had been wordless."

Anandamayee Ma was always extremely respectful and deferential in the presence of mahatmas, often referring to herself as a simple, uneducated child. But this did not in any way inhibit her from asking them direct and penetrating questions, particularly if she did not agree with them on a particular point.

In this description of their meeting, and particularly in the portrayal of their different responses to dealing with the public, is revealed an essential difference between Anandamayee Ma and J. Krishnamurti. Anandamayee Ma made no distinction whatsoever between herself and those bowing before her. She saw everything as "God interacting with God" as she would sometimes say. In any case, to bow before a respected and revered figure in India is as common a gesture of elementary respect as shaking hands in the West.

Anandamayee Ma had no desire to do away with tradition but on the contrary wanted to revitalize it, bringing out the fundamental spirituality upon which it was originally based. She often pointed out that in the act of bowing down (making pranam), particularly to an exalted spiritual personage, a profound transmission of spiritual energy takes place —something utterly beyond the mind that is the antithesis of anything debasing or humbling.

Excerpted from "Death Must Die", the diaries of Atmananda by Ram Alexander published by Indica Book, Varanasi, India

*　　*　　*

Ramakrishna Parmahamsa

Ramakrishna Parmahamsa (1836-1886) was born in a poor Brahmin family in a small town near Calcutta, West Bengal. As a young man, he was artistic and a popular storyteller and actor.

Young Ramakrishna was prone to experiences of spiritual reverie and temporary loss of consciousness. His early spiritual experiences included going into a state of rapture while watching the flight of cranes, and losing consciousness of the outer world while playing the role of the god Shiva in a school play.

In 1866, he became a priest at a temple to the Goddess Kali located near Calcutta on the Ganges River. He spent increasing amounts of time giving offerings and meditating on her. At one point he became frustrated, feeling he could not live any longer without seeing Kali. He demanded that the goddess appear to him. He threatened to take his own life with a ritual dagger (normally held in the hand of the Kali statue). At this point, he explained how the goddess appeared to him as an ocean of light.

Ramakrishna practiced the rituals of many religions, and found that they all brought him to the same divine reality in the end.

Contact for details: www.belurmath.org

* * *

27. Mother's pleasure lies in playing with Her creation

Ramakrishna Paramhamsa

The Divine Mother is always playful and sportive. This universe is Her play. She is self-willed and must always have Her own way. She is full of bliss. She gives freedom to one out of a hundred thousand.

A Devotee: "But, sir, if She likes, She can give freedom to all. Why, then, has She kept us bound to the world?"

Master: "That is Her will. She wants to continue playing with Her created beings. In a game of hide-and-seek the running about soon stops if in the beginning all the players touch the 'granny'. If all touch her, then how can the game go on? That displeases her. Her pleasure is in continuing the game.

"It is as if the Divine Mother said to the human mind in confidence, with a sign from Her eye, 'Go and enjoy the world.' How can one blame the mind?

The mind can disentangle itself from worldliness if, through Her grace, She makes it turn toward Herself. Only then does it become devoted to the Lotus Feet of the Divine Mother."

Devotee: "Sir, can't we realize God without complete renunciation?"

Master: "Of course you can! Why should you renounce everything? You are all right as you are, following the middle path-like molasses, partly solid and partly liquid. Do you know the game of nax? Having scored the maximum number of points, I am out of the game. I can't enjoy it. But you are very clever. Some of you have scored ten points, some six, and some five. You have scored just the right number; so you are not out of the game like me. The game can go on. Why, that's fine!

"I tell you the truth: there is nothing wrong in your being in the world. But you must direct your mind toward God; otherwise you will not succeed. Do your duty with one hand and with the other hold to God. After the duty is over, you will hold to God with both hands.

Bondage & liberation are of the mind

"It is all a question of the mind. Bondage and liberation are of the mind alone. The mind will take the color you dye it with. It is like white clothes just returned from the laundry. If you dip them in red dye, they will be red.

If you dip them in blue or green, they will be blue or green. They will take only the color you dip them in.

Haven't you noticed that, if you read a little English, you at once begin to utter English words: Foot fut it mit? Then you put on boots and whistle a tune, and so on. It all goes together. Or, if a scholar studies Sanskrit, he will at once rattle off Sanskrit verses. If you are in bad company, then you will talk and think like your companions. On the other hand, when you are in the company of devotees, you will think and talk only of God.

"The mind is everything. A man has his wife on one side and his daughter on the other. He shows his affection to them in different ways. But his mind is one and the same.

"Bondage is of the mind, and freedom is also of the mind. A man is free if he constantly thinks: 'I am a free soul. How can I be bound, whether I live in the world or in the forest? I am a child of God, the King of Kings. If bitten by a snake, a man may get rid of its venom by saying emphatically, 'There is no poison in me.' In the same way, by repeating with grit and determination, 'I am not bound, I am free', one really becomes free.

Excerpted from The Gospel of Sri Ramakrishna by M.

*　　*　　*

Ram Dass

Ram Dass (Richard Alpert) was born in 1931 to a Jewish family in Newton, Massachusetts. He was a prominent Harvard psychologist and psychedelic pioneer with Dr. Timothy Leary. He continued his psychedelic research until that fateful Eastern trip in 1967, when he traveled to India where he met his guru, Neem Karoli Baba, affectionately known as *Maharajji*, who gave Ram Dass his name, which means *"servant of God."* Everything changed then – his intense dharmic life started, and he became a pivotal influence on a culture that has reverberated with the words "Be Here Now" ever since.

Since 1968, Ram Dass has pursued a panoramic array of spiritual methods and practices from potent ancient wisdom traditions. His unique skill in getting people to cut through and feel divine love without dogma is still a positive influence on many people from all over the planet.

Asked to sum up his life's message, he says, "I help people as a way to work on myself, and I work on myself to help people."

Ram Dass now resides on Maui, Hawaii, where he shares his teachings through the internet and through retreats on Maui.

Contact for details: www.ramdass.org

* * *

28. Maharajji gone – Does it make any difference?

Ram Dass

During the summer of 1973 I was staying at my father's farm in New Hampshire, and was there in September when the telegram arrived. My father and my stepmother, looking rather concerned, met me when I returned from shopping at the village. Dad said, "This telegram just came from India, don't understand it, but I copied it down word for word as the operator gave it to me."

"At 1:15, September 11, Babaji left his bojhay (sic) in Vrindaban . . ." The telegram went on with further details. My father asked, "What does it mean?"

"It means," I said, "that Maharaji died."

They immediately tried to console or at least commiserate with me, but their words seemed strangely irrelevant, for I felt absolutely nothing – neither sad nor happy. There was no sense of loss. Perhaps I was just numb. A couple with marital difficulties were waiting for me, so I went and sat with them and helped them unwind the tangle of thread of their loves and hatreds.

Every now and then in the midst of the discussion, my mind would wander and I'd think, "Maharajji isn't in his body. Isn't that strange," or "I wonder what will happen now?" But I pushed such thoughts aside and forced my consciousness back to the task at hand, for, whatever was to come, there was no sense in stopping service to others.

Throughout that day and many times thereafter I remembered the words of the great Ramana Maharshi. He was dying of cancer and in the past had shown power to heal others, and his devotees were now begging him to heal himself. He kept refusing, and they cried, "Don't leave us, don't leave us," to which he replied, "Don't be silly. Where could I go?"

After all, where could Maharajji go? I had him in my heart. I had been living with him moment by moment and yet not with his physical presence – so did it really make any difference? I wasn't sure.

When the couple left I started calling other devotees in the United States and Canada and asked them to call others. It was agreed that those within a radius of three or four hundred miles would join me in New Hampshire. By the next noon some twenty of us were gathered. It was a peculiar meeting.

We were all somewhat dumbfounded by the news and many were crying, but at the same time we were happy to be together and felt Maharaji's presence very strongly with us. We cooked a big meal, which we ate around the fire. But before the food we went up to my room to sit before the puja table and meditate and do arti.

While all of us sang the ancient Sanskrit prayer, we took turns offering the light (in the form of a candle flame) by waving it before Maharaji's picture. After my turn I went to the back of the group and watched. In the reflection of the candlelight I looked at the faces of my guru brothers and sisters and saw their expressions of love and the purity of their hearts. And finally I was able to cry – not out of sadness at the loss, but rather because of the presence of pure and perfect love that is Maharaji and which I felt in this gathering of hearts.

Excerpted from *Miracle of Love: Stories about Neem Karoli Baba*

*   *   *

Section Eight

INTERNAL, EXTERNAL

Modern psychology says that anger is normal and that one must be angry if a particular situation warrants it. Similarly, there is "normal" jealousy and "normal" sadness. Because they are "normal," there is nothing wrong with them. Swami Dayananda Saraswati says that in Vedanta, there is no such thing as "normal" sorrow. The use of the word "normal," then, marks the difference between a psychological and a spiritual problem. Vedanta can resolve a problem if the mind is more or less normal. But, if the mind is abnormal, Vedanta cannot help because the person cannot handle the subject matter.

A superficial approach to anything lands one in trouble. So, "Eat, drink and make merry" is a very shallow view of life. We get enchanted by the world of names and forms. But we feel horrified or dejected by what happens sometimes in this very world. Swami Tejomayananda says what is visible is only an appearance and we all know that appearances are deceptive. The one truth that is not visible is subtle and it is this Truth that will solve all the problems. To see this Truth, we need a pure mind and subtle intellect.

Speaking from his own experience, Colin Drake says all motion arises in stillness, exists in stillness, is known by its comparison with stillness, and eventually subsides back into stillness. For example, if you walk across a room, before you start there is stillness, as you walk the room is still and you know you are moving relative to this stillness, and when you stop once again there is stillness. In the same way every 'thing' (consciousness in motion) arises in awareness (consciousness at rest), exists in awareness, is known in awareness and subsides back into awareness.

* * *

Swami Dayananda Saraswati

Swami Dayananda Saraswati was born as Natarajan in Manjakudi—Thiruvarur district of Tamil Nadu on August 15, 1930. He became interested in Vedanta after listening to the public talks of Swami Chinmayananda in the years 1952-53. Becoming actively involved with the then newly formed Chinmaya Mission, he was given Sannyasa by Swami Chinmayananda in 1962 and given the name Swami Dayananda Saraswati.

Swami Dayananda is a quintessential teacher and a revered scholar of Vedanta. He has been teaching Vedanta in India for more than four decades, and around the world since 1976. In his public talks abroad, Swamiji has spoken at many of the most prestigious American universities, and has addressed international conventions, UNESCO and the United Nations, where he participated in the Millennium Peace Summit.

Swamiji has founded the Arsha Vidya Pitham in Rishikesh, the Arsha Vidya Gurukulam at Coimbatore and the Arsha Vijnana Gurukulam at Nagpur. In the U.S., the main center is the Arsha Vidya Gurukulam at Saylorsburg, Pennsylvania. The graduates from these courses are now acharyas, teaching around the world. More than one hundred are now Swamis and are highly respected as scholars and teachers throughout India and abroad.

Contact for details: www.arshavidya.in

*   *   *

29. Difference between a spiritual & a psychological problem

Swami Dayananda Saraswati

Question: Swamiji, how can we tell the difference between a deep spiritual problem and a psychological problem?

Answer: An example of psychological problem, I would say, is finding that I am sad for no reason. Or, suddenly, I find I am panicky. Or, if there is something a little strange or overwhelming, I feel threatened. Perhaps I cannot be in crowds. I shy away from people. Or I may be afraid of authority which may be connected to some childhood problems or some parental problems. These are all psychological problems.

A spiritual problem is seen in someone who has solved all these psychological problems, for the most part, but who is still sad. He or she is considered to be "normal," can interact well with people and so on, but is subject to his or her own yo-yo emotions – now high, now low. This is because down below, there is always a self-image which is as good as the body-mind-sense complex.

How then are we going to solve the problem? There is a legitimate fear, legitimate anger, legitimate sorrow – "legitimate" because society has accepted them as legitimate. Modern psychology says that anger is normal and that one must be angry if a particular situation warrants it.

Similarly, there is "normal" jealousy and "normal" sadness. Because they are "normal," there is nothing wrong with them. These we solve spiritually.

Vedanta says there is no such thing as "normal" sorrow. The use of the word "normal," then, marks the difference between psychological and a spiritual problem.

Vedanta can resolve a problem if the mind is more or less normal. But, if the mind is abnormal, Vedanta cannot help because the person cannot handle the subject matter. It will not take hold. If, however, the person is unable to grasp what Vedanta is saying, but stays with it and follows all the attitudes and values properly, then it can help.

Vedanta itself has its own approach to psychology, normal psychology, that is. It is räga-dvesha (likes and dislikes) psychology and includes prayer, meditation, and an understanding of values. If a person stays with it, follows it all properly, it can help. I consider this to be the best approach.

On the other hand, Vedanta has no answer for abnormal psychology. It cannot help people who are schizophrenic, for example. It will only confuse them, in fact, and is therefore detrimental. This is why, originally in India, and still today, there are those who will not teach Vedanta to just anyone.

Only when the guru is satisfied that the mind is prepared will he teach the person.

It was a common practice, one that is still used today, that when a man with unprepared mind came to a teacher in Rishikesh, in the north of India, the teacher would send him on foot, to Rameswaram, which is in the deep south. He was told to go and come back – without money. "Then I will teach you," the teacher would say. The idea was that by the time he came back, he would be normal – if he came back.

Excerpted from www.avgsatsang.com

* * *

Swami Tejomayananda

Born into a Maharashtrian family on June 30, 1950, in Madhya Pradesh, India, Sudhakar Kaitwade was not spiritually inclined. At the age of 20, a year away from getting his Master's degree in Physics, he attended a talk by Swami Chinmayananda on Bhagavad Gita and his life changed. He joined Chinmaya Mission course and in 1983, Swami Chinmayananda initiated him into sannyasa, bestowing upon him the name, Swami Tejomayananda.

Swami Tejomayananda was posted to Chinmaya Mission's U.S. Centre in San Jose, California, where he remained as acharya until 1993. After Swami Chinmayananda attained Mahasamadhi he became the Head of Chinmaya Mission Worldwide.

Swami Tejomayananda has continuously and dynamically pursued his guru's grand spiritual and organizational vision. Progressive in thinking and precise in decision-making, he has inspired and executed many notable, innovative projects, including the Chinmaya International Residential School in Coimbatore, the Chinmaya Centre of World Understanding in New Delhi, the Chinmaya International Foundation near Cochin, the Chinmaya Heritage Centre in Chennai, the expansion of the Chinmaya Mission Hospital in Bangalore and the Chinmaya Vibhooti Vision Centre near Pune.

Always jovial, smiling, and welcoming, he is readily accessible.

Contact for details: chinmayamission.com

* * *

30. The invisible is more significant than what is visible

Swami Tejomayananda

At a satsang in one place, someone asked me: "How to have fun in life?"

"Be serious", I said, and I said it rather seriously because really speaking the pursuit of happiness is a serious matter. A superficial approach to anything lands one in trouble. So,

"Eat, drink and make merry" is a very shallow view of life. Deeper enquiry takes us to deeper truths.

Let us see how Vedanta views the issue of happiness. To put it in a simple way, life is constituted of perception and response. Whether we like it or not, we cannot help responding to people, to situations, to events, in general to the world around. Now, response depends on individual perception.

Everybody sees the same object but how each sees it makes all the difference. Perception therefore can be called as a vision of life and response as an action or reaction that depends on this vision.

Superficially whatever we see or experience with our gross sense organs is alone considered as real. No wonder, one finds the world very enchanting with its infinite variety and matchless beauty. But when we try to understand the same world a little deeply, it becomes very mind-boggling.

Normally what happens is we get enchanted by the world of names and forms. But again we feel horrified or dejected by what happens sometimes in this very world. All this proves that what is visible is immaterial, what is invisible is much more significant.

What is visible is only an appearance and we all know that appearances are deceptive. The one truth that is not visible is subtle and it is this Truth that will solve all the problems. To see this Truth, we need a pure mind and subtle intellect.

But sadly, many of us do not have this kind of a vision. We are stuck either with rājasika vision (extroverted outlook) or a tāmasika vision (dull approach). Lord Krishna in the Gītā explains the pitfalls inherent in these approaches.

For example, a person with rājasika vision sees differences while perceiving the work and he considers those differences alone as real. He forms mental division such as "I—my", "you—yours", "good—bad" and so on. The actions performed by him therefore are born of either attachment or aversion. He is happy only as long as everything runs according to his tastes and preferences. The moment something goes awry, he becomes agitated and troubled.

A person with a tāmasika vision is even worse. He is deeply, fanatically and exclusively attached to a particular object, ideology or cause, with the result that even the happiness he experiences reflects his conflict. His happiness is got by unhealthy means as fights, addiction, sleep and indolence.

Therefore, it becomes clear that the sāttvika kind of happiness alone deserves to be pursued.

The Upanishads praise a person with a sāttvika vision as someone with a balanced view of life as he has eliminated sorrow, delusion and hatred once and for all. All of us are seeking this kind of happiness.

All other ways to attain happiness are illusory, both at individual and the collective level.

Excerpted from Vision of Life, www.chinmayamission.com

*   *   *

Colin Drake

Colin Drake has been seeking the Truth since he was born in 1948, and has been meditating since 1978. Early on he found that the so-called Christians were not interested in practicing what Christ taught. In 1965, living in central London, he experimented with hallucinogens, finding them beneficial for opening his subconscious although he does not recommend these for everybody. The psychedelic states gave a glimpse of mystical states which he suspected were attainable through spiritual practices.

There followed a few years of investigating various spiritual paths. In Sydney, he was initiated into the worship, *japa* (mantra repetition) of Ramakrishna which he continued quite happily for ten years.

In 1996 he encountered a disciple of Ramana Maharshi, Gangaji, who said: 'Stop! Be still, you are already That'. The message being that the effort and search were masking that which is always present; all that was required was to 'stop' and see what is always here. This news came like a breath of fresh air and he glimpsed the essence, that undeniable ever-present reality.

Ever since he has been writing many articles and poems, based on meditations, contemplations and answers to questions, then collated into books. He lives in Sydney, Australia, with his wife Janet who is a studio production potter and qualified yoga teacher.

Contact for details: www.lulu.com

*   *   *

31. External world is a mixture of thoughts & sensations

Colin Drake

Non-duality is simply 'not two' (of anything). In fact the term 'nonmultiplicity' would be more accurate for what is being suggested here is 'not many' rather than 'not two'.

What we are trying to get a handle on here is that there is actually no (permanently existing) thing in existence, and that all apparent 'things' are manifestations of the same essence.

This can be shown by investigating the nature of our own subjective experiences, which is actually all that any of us have to investigate. For each of us any external object or thing is experienced as a combination of thought (including mental images) and sensation, i.e. you may see it, touch it, know what it is called, and so on . . . Thus everything in the external world is experienced as a mixture of thoughts and sensations, and when we attempt to investigate any 'thing' it is these that we are investigating.

In any given moment of direct experience there are only three elements: thoughts (including all mental images), sensations (everything detected by the senses) and awareness of these thoughts and sensations. All thoughts and sensations are ephemeral objects (the perceived) which appear in this awareness (the perceiver) which is the constant subject. So at a deeper level than the ever-changing objects (thoughts and sensations) we are this constant subject, awareness itself.

To put this in a slightly different way, we can easily notice that every thought and sensation occurs in awareness, exists in awareness and dissolves back into awareness. Before any particular thought or sensation there is effortless awareness of 'what is': the sum of all thoughts and sensations occurring at any given instant. During the thought or sensation in question there is effortless awareness of it within 'what is'. Then when it has gone there is still effortless awareness of 'what is'.

In our direct experience everything arises in, exists in and subsides back into awareness itself.

Awareness can also be defined as universal consciousness when it is totally at rest, completely still; aware of every movement that is occurring within it. In our direct experience we can see that awareness is still, as there is awareness of the slightest movement of mind or body. In fact this is the 'stillness' relative to which any movement can be known.

Every 'thing' that is occurring in consciousness is a manifestation of cosmic energy, for the string theory and the earlier theory of relativity show that matter is in fact energy, which is consciousness in motion (or motion in consciousness). For energy is synonymous with motion and consciousness is the substratum, or deepest level, of all existence.

Now all motion arises in stillness, exists in stillness, is known by its comparison with stillness, and eventually subsides back into stillness. For example, if you walk across a room, before you start there is stillness, as you walk the room is still and you know you are moving relative to this stillness, and when you stop once again there is stillness. In the same way every 'thing' (consciousness in motion) arises in awareness (consciousness at rest), exists in awareness, is known in awareness and subsides back into awareness. Awareness is still, but is the container of all potential energy which is continually bubbling up into manifestation (physical energy) and then subsiding back into stillness.

Thus there is no dichotomy or duality between the physical world and 'awareness' for they are both manifestations of the same essence. The physical universe is just cosmic energy (consciousness in motion) when it is manifest into physical form, and awareness (consciousness at rest) contains this same energy in latent form as potential energy. Therefore there is in reality no multiplicity (nonduality) as there is only consciousness existing in two modes, in motion and at rest.

Excerpted from www.nonduality.com

*   *   *

Adi Shankaracharya

One of the greatest philosophers of India, Adi Shankaracharya founded Advaita Vedanta, which is one of the sub-schools of Vedanta. He believed in the concept of the Vedas but at the same time advocated against the rituals and religious practices that were over exaggerated.

Shankara was born in a very poor family in 788 A.D. in a village named Kaladi in Kerala, India. Right from childhood he showed a penchant for spiritual knowledge. He could easily recite the Puranas and the Epics and mastered the Vedas during his early years in Gurukul.

Under his guru Govinda Bhagavatpada, Shankaracharya gained expertise in different forms of Yoga and knowledge of Brahma. Shankara spread the tenets of Advaita Vedanta, the supreme philosophy of monism to the four corners of

India. He established four 'mutts' or monastic centers in four corners of India. The mutts are Jyothir Mutt at Badrinath in northern India; Sarada Mutt at Sringeri in southern India; Govardhan Mutt at Jaganath Puri in eastern India and Kalika Mutt at Dwarka in western India.

It is believed that Shankara attained heavenly abode in Kedarnath and was only 32 years old when he died.

Contact for details: www.sringeri.net

*　*　*

32. True nature is internal, unattached & free from action

Adi Shankaracharya

To be free from bondage the wise man must practice discrimination between self and non-self. By that alone he will become full of joy, recognizing himself as Being, Consciousness and Bliss.

Just as one separates a blade of grass from its sheaths, so by discriminating one's true nature as internal, unattached and free from action, and abandoning all else, one is free and identified only with one's true self.

This body is the product of food, and constitutes the material sheath. It depends on food and dies without it. It is a mass of skin, flesh, blood, bones and uncleanness. It is not fit to see as oneself, who is ever pure.

The body did not exist before birth, nor will it exist after death. It is born for a moment, its qualities are momentary, and it is inherently changing. It is not a single thing, but inert, and should be viewed like an earthen pot. How could it be one's true self, which is the observer of changing phenomena?

Made up of arms and legs and so on, the body cannot be one's true self as it can live on without various limbs, and other faculties persist without them. What is controlled cannot be the controller.

While the body of the observer is of a specific nature, behavior and situation, it is clear that the nature of one's true self is devoid of characteristics.

How could the body, which is a heap of bones, covered with flesh, full of filth and highly impure, be oneself, the featureless observer?

The deluded man makes the assumption that he is the mass of skin, flesh, fat bones and filth, while the man who is strong in discrimination knows himself as devoid of characteristics, the innate supreme Reality.

'I am the body' is the opinion of the fool. 'I am body and soul' is the view of the scholar, while for the great-souled, discriminating man, his inner knowledge is 'I am God'.

Get rid of the opinion of yourself as this mass of skin, flesh, fat, bones and filth, foolish one, and make yourself instead the self of everything, the God beyond all thought, and enjoy supreme peace.

While the scholar does not overcome his sense of 'I am this' in the body and its faculties, there is no liberation for him, however much he may be learned in religion and philosophy.

Just as you have no self identification with your shadow-body, reflection-body, dream-body or imagination-body, so you should not have with the living body either.

Identification of oneself with the body is the seed of the pain of birth etc. in people attached to the unreal, so get rid of it with care. When this thought is eliminated, there is no more desire for rebirth.

The vital energy joined to the five activities forms the vitality sheath, by which the material sheath is filled, and engages in all these activities.

The Breath, being a product of the vital energy, is not one's true nature either. Like the air, it enters and leaves the body, and knows neither its own or other people's good or bad, dependent as it is on something else.

The faculty of knowledge and the mind itself constitute the mind-made sheath, the cause of such distinctions as 'me' and 'mine'. It is strong and has the faculty of creating distinctions of perception etc., and works itself through the vitality sheath.

The mind-made fire burns the multiplicity of experience in the fuel of numerous desires of the senses presented as oblations in the form of sense objects by the five senses like five priests.

There is no such thing as ignorance beyond the thinking mind. Thought is itself ignorance, the cause of the bondage of becoming. When thought is eliminated, everything else is eliminated. When thought increases everything else increases.

Excerpted from Crest Jewel of Wisdom (Viveka-Chudamani) translated by Rev. John Henry Richards and placed on website Realization.org

*   *   *

Section Nine

DESIRE, THOUGHT

When a desire is fulfilled the personal 'I' is happy for a while. This happiness arises because of the absence of desire and has nothing to do with the properties of the object of desire. Jac O'Keeffe says original perfection is restored when desire is not running. If you imagine yourself to be separate from the world then the world will appear as separate from you, and you will experience desire and fear.

Ramesh Balsekar says if you meditate without expectation, then there is no problem. What happens is you sit in meditation and all the time you expect something to happen – call it silence, call it being in oneness, or whatever. What you call it doesn't matter. But the problem arises if you meditate with an expectation. So if there is no expectation, you live your life. Whatever happens. Why not let life happen, he asks.

In Uddhava Gita, Lord Krishna says, the man of knowledge, though has a body, is not conditioned by it any more than a dreamer just awakened from the dream is unaffected by the experiences of his dream. "The man of ignorance assumes that he is the doer of all actions which are actually done by organs of action and perception." Krishna says, he is really free who remains unaffected though his senses feed on objects of senses.

Talking of renunciation, Mahatma Gandhi says that from the standpoint of pure Truth, the body too is a possession. The desire for enjoyment creates bodies for the soul. When this desire vanishes, there remains no further need for the body, and man is free from the vicious cycle of births and deaths. "The soul is omnipresent; why should she care to be confined within the cage-like body, or do evil and even kill for the sake of the cage," he asserts.

* * *

Jac O'Keeffe

Jac O'Keeffe, raised in rural Ireland, led a "normal life" until the age of 30 years when a sixth sense awakening brought her face to face with the non-physical world. O'Keeffe's life changed and a busy healing practice developed.

Through her innate ability to see chakras, energy fields, auras and to speak to those who had passed from this life, O'Keeffe's clients were able to find meaning in their lives and let go of past hurts that held them back from their own spiritual development and perfect peace.

She worked for seven years as a spiritual teacher, and her personal quest led to that which is beyond the mind – transcending dualistic thought.

Through her work, Jac found that her clients' depression and emotional pain were caused by a quest for meaning and value: a spiritual yearning rather than a bio-chemical imbalance.

Furthering her own spiritual practice she left her work and her life in Ireland to live in Spain, then India, spending much time in solitude, silence and in meditation.

Jac holds weekend Satsangs and residential retreats. Her book, Born to be Free, skillfully leads the reader to the state of stillness, harmony and peace.

Contact for details: www.jac-okeeffe.com

33. The state of craving inhibits deeper experience

Jac O'Keeffe

All desire arises from an innate lack of contentment. While nothing that mind can imagine and want is of any real value, the personal 'I' will ensure that each day is peppered with efforts to fulfill desires. In fact when identified thought is running, there is interest in little else. It is the nature of desire to prompt the mind to create a world for its fulfillment.

The state of craving for anything inhibits deeper experience. When mind is fixated on a desire, maturation is arrested. If you inquire into yourself, all you really desire is desirelessness. Desirelessness can be recognized as the moment of satisfaction when desire is fulfilled. There is calmness, perfection and a feeling of completeness.

Desire for an object or experience is a compensation for the lack of fulfillment of the ultimate desire – desirelessness. There is no end to the cyclical nature of desire; however, the cycle falls away when it is seen to be a looped pattern of thinking. The perpetuation of desire is predicated on the fact that personal 'I' desires the very thing that cannot come by desire. The smallest desire has the ability to ignite a long line of action as one objective idea feeds the next.

To engage in desire is a lack of discrimination; let it be seen that acquiring objects, be it a car or a lover, can never bring you to the end of desire. In order for you to enjoy something it must first be objectified by mind as an independent form or formless experience.

There is only movement in consciousness which we call life force or functioning and we give names to create an objectified world. Then if this apparent division into subject-object is taken to be true, the desires to have and to own, to acquire and enjoy, will follow. Thus the mind will make the body dance to its tunes.

When a desire is fulfilled the personal 'I' is happy for a while. This happiness arises because of the absence of desire and has nothing to do with the properties of the object of desire. Original perfection is restored when desire is not running. If you imagine yourself to be separate from the world then the world will appear as separate from you, and you will experience desire and fear. As long as there is identification with the body, attractions and repulsions will operate.

You cannot but see the world through the ideas you have about yourself.

Managing desire has nothing to do with your relationships with objects of desire; it is your own misunderstanding that requires correction. Find out how the perception of objects arises in mind and do not follow thought patterns in ignorance.

There is no object which is of a different nature from the subject, and as there is only the subject, how can it be seen as an object? Let it be realized that there is only subject and then it is clear that there can be no division in such a vision. All experience rests on the reality of objects. If you investigate you will find that objects are unreal.

Thus the effect of an unreal object is also non-existent and the experience of any effect is delusion. Let the end of desire and experience come into view through correct seeing. Understand that the world has no real existence and it will no longer be troublesome.

It can be said that desire is the memory of pleasure and that fear is the memory of pain. These are simply habits of mind. Once you know they are impermanent and not real, why bother with them? Pull attention away from the personal and impersonal, and all of this is just the flickering of energy.

Excerpted from 'From Awakening to Liberation,' Chapter 3

*　　*　　*

Ramesh S. Balsekar

Ramesh S. Balsekar (1917 –2009) was a well-educated young man at the London School of Economics. After working his way up the corporate ladder, he served as General Manager of the Bank of India in Bombay. During his early life, Ramesh always felt he was enacting some role in a play that must, and would, end soon. Deep within, he believed that there had to be more to life than merely getting ahead of the other man.

The answer came soon after his retirement when he had an encounter, which soon led to daily meetings, with the well-known sage, and his Guru, Sri Nisargadatta Maharaj. For Ramesh the total understanding that 'no one does anything' happened in 1979. Ramesh began translating most of the daily talks held by Nisargadatta Maharaj.

He himself began teaching in 1982. The 'command' to talk was given by his Guru, he says. The number of visitors who came to listen to Ramesh began to grow. Since then, he has written many books and held several seminars in Europe and the USA. He continued to give discourse and answer questions in his Mumbai home until shortly before his death.

Contact for details: www.rameshbalsekar.com

34. Expectation is the whole problem in life

Ramesh Balsekar

The trouble is expectation. That is the whole problem in life. You expect something, you don't get it, you feel frustrated. Money is really the main problem for most people. I personally think one should not lessen the importance of money. If money is no problem, 80 percent of the problems are not there.

Then what remains as problems are what the mind creates out of expectation. If the expectation doesn't materialize there is frustration. So if it is possible to live without expectation, then there is no frustration.

If you meditate without expectation, then there is no problem. I'm not asking you not to meditate, but meditate without any expectation. Now what happens is you sit in meditation and all the time you expect something to happen – call it silence, call it being in oneness, or whatever. What you call it doesn't matter. But the problem arises if you meditate with an expectation.

So if there is no expectation, you live your life. Whatever happens. Why not let life happen? I can't say this to someone who needs money, who needs money to live, for the family. Talking about spirituality to a hungry man is like adding insult to injury. I can't tell him or her to do something and not expect money. That's why I never underestimate the importance of money. If money is not a problem, then why have any expectations?

Let life happen.

Legan: I feel I have to grow. I have to change, I have to become . . .

Ramesh: That's the whole point! Why?

Legan: I have to become more spiritual . . .

Ramesh: Why?

Legan: . . . or more open, more centered or . . .

Ramesh: That's what I'm saying. So try to live your life or let life happen without expecting anything. The expectation happens because you're bored. The mind is empty, and the thinking mind never allows itself to be empty. The thinking mind always wants something.

That's why the thinking occurs and the expectations happen. If you don't have to earn money, then do something to give the working mind a change – do something to help people. There must be something you can do to help people around you who need help. So if boredom is your problem . . . .

Legan: There is always this talking in this fellowship that I'm going to. There's always this talking about transformation and change, and I feel nothing is happening with me. Sometimes it's okay. Sometimes I feel I have to do something.

Ramesh: So do it. That is exactly what I'm telling you. And do it without expecting anything. And having done something and satisfaction arises – fine. If it doesn't arise – that is also fine.

Legan: Is meditating everyday helpful?

Ramesh: Helpful for what? That's the whole problem. Meditation is helpful for what?

Legan: For peace of mind

Ramesh: Ah! So it is peace of mind that you are looking for, isn't it? And that is the expectation.

Legan: I think I'm always looking for something.

Ramesh: Yes. That is the whole problem. So keep yourself busy doing something, and if you don't need to do anything for money, so much the better. But do something. I'm sure you can't say that there are no people who need some kind of help.

Excerpted from pages 144-146 'Who Cares?!' published by Zen Publications

*   *   *

Uddhava Gita

Krishna spoke the Uddhava Gita to Uddhava, a devotee and a dear friend, shortly before he left the world. Uddhava was perplexed to see the impending destruction of the Yadava community, in which Krishna was also brought up.

Krishna explained: "Made insolent by prowess, heroism and fortune, and inclined to take possession of the whole world, this celebrated race has been kept in check by Me. If I depart without destroying the huge race of the Yadus, who have grown insolent, the entire humanity will meet its destruction . . ." Greatly saddened, Uddhava beseeched Krishna to take him also. In reply Krishna then expounded the Uddhava Gita, which is part of Bhagavata Purana.

These teachings of Krishna to Uddddhava are spread over 23 chapters – from the 7th to 29th – of the 11th Skandha (Canto) of Srimad Bhagavatam. These teachings are also called Hamsa Gita. The 11th Canto ends with the final destruction of the Yadavas by mutual fighting and the exit of Krishna after being shot at by a hunter.

Contact for details: srimadbhagavatam.com

35. Brooding over sensory objects creates passion

Uddhava Gita

Krishna clarifies (in Uddhava Gita) the characterization of a jiva as bound or emancipated is determined by its being subject to or not subject to the Gunas of Prakriti controlled by the Lord himself and has nothing to do with its essential nature. It is like experiencing happiness or sorrow in a dream which ceases on waking.

"So long as there is ignorance Jiva is taken to suffer the bodily sufferings which get cleared once the individual realizes the knowledge of the Self.

The man of knowledge, though has a body, is not conditioned by it any more than a dreamer just awakened from the dream is unaffected by the experiences of his dream.

"The man of ignorance assumes that he is the doer of all actions which are actually done by organs of action and perception. He is really free who remains unaffected though his senses feed on objects of senses.

"If a man becomes a scholar in the scriptures but does not practice and become one with the Self is as useless as keeping a cow which does not give milk or an unchaste wife. A wise man who always chants the name of the Lord and hears his stories will surely attain to his state."

Extinction of the "I" sense

Uddhava remarked that most men know that the sensuous pleasures are baneful in their results, inviting endless troubles, yet like dogs, donkeys and goats they heartily plunge into them and asked why it is so.

The Lord answered: "It all begins with perverse sense of "I" which causes Rajo Guna to invade the mind and induces it to conceive the objects of enjoyment and the means of enjoying them. Brooding over such sensory objects creates an uncontrollable passion for them which overwhelms the mind and impels irrevocable actions.

"Although the perception of their evil consequences of such actions is present, the impetuosity of the passion is too strong to arrest them. But the man of discrimination exerts hard to control his infatuation and thus spares himself from the suffering. Such a man will turn his mind to me, away from everything else, and will be finally established in me.

Path of Devotion

Uddhava asks Krishna:" Various ways of liberation have been taught by various teachers. You also teach the path of devotion. Are all these ways equally good?"

Krishna replies: "Many are the means described for the attainment of the highest good, such as love, performance of duty, self-control, truthfulness, sacrifices, gifts, austerity, charity, vows, observance of moral precepts etc.

But of all these the path of love and devotion to me is the best.

"To the man who finds delight in me alone, who is self-controlled and even minded, having no longing in his heart for anything other than me, the whole universe is full of bliss. Such a devotee who has surrendered himself to the Lord does not even desire salvation and finds bliss in me alone; this devotee is very dear to me. His happiness is unconditional.

"Although he may not be a master of senses, he is not a servant to them, either. As fire kindled into a blaze burns the wood to ashes, devotion to me completely consumes all evil.

Neither by the study of scriptures nor by Yoga or by any other method could I be easily attained. I, the Self, dear to the devotee am attainable by love and devotion. Devotion purifies even the lowliest of the low.

Without love for me virtues and learning are unfruitful. He who loves me is made pure and is a purifying influence upon the whole universe. Let not your mind run after worldly things. Give your mind to me, meditate upon me."

Then Krishna teaches Uddhava the process of meditating upon him.

Excerpted from esamskriti.com from an essay by TN Sethumadhavan tnsethu@rediffmail.com

*   *   *

Mahatma Gandhi

Mahatma (Great Soul) Mohandas Karamchand Gandhi (1869-1948) stands as one of history's greatest heroes of "engaged spirituality," a spirituality that is active within the world to help heal injustice, hatred, pettiness, fear and violence with justice, loving-kindness, equanimity, courage and nonviolence. Employing non-violent civil disobedience, Gandhi led India to independence and inspired movements for civil rights and freedom across the world.

As a pioneer of Satyagraha, or resistance through mass non-violent civil disobedience, he became one of the major political and spiritual leaders of his time. Satyagraha remains one of the most potent philosophies in freedom struggles throughout the world today.

For Gandhi, morality and religion were synonymous. He made it clear that what he wanted to achieve was self-realization, "to see God face to face, to attain Moksha". It was his faith in spirituality that gave him the courage to act the way he did on so many occasions, even when it looked as if he was treading a lonely path.

Though Gandhi was a lawyer, politician, and revolutionary, he acknowledged that his most powerful weapon was prayer. Through his daily meditation, he came to believe in the presence and nearness of God in day-to-day life.

Contact for details: www.mkgandhi.org

36. Civilization consists in voluntary reduction of wants

Mahatma Gandhi

Civilization, in the real sense of the term, consists not in the multiplication, but in the deliberate and voluntary reduction of wants. This alone promotes real happiness and contentment, and increases the capacity for service.

From the standpoint of pure Truth, the body too is a possession.

It has been truly said, that desire for enjoyment creates bodies for the soul. When this desire vanishes, there remains no further need for the body, and man is free from the vicious cycle of births and deaths. The soul is omnipresent; why should she care to be confined within the cage-like body, or do evil and even kill for the sake of the cage?

We thus arrive at the ideal of total renunciation, and learn to use the body for the purposes of service so long as it exists, so much so that service, and not bread, becomes with us the staff of life. We eat and drink, sleep and awake, for service alone. Such an attitude of mind brings us real happiness and the beatific vision in the fullness of time. Let us examine ourselves from this standpoint.

We should remember that Non-possession is a principle applicable to thoughts, as well as to things. One, who fills his brain with useless knowledge, violates that inestimable principle. Thoughts, which turn us away from God, or do not turn us towards Him, constitute impediments in our way.

In this connection we may consider the definition of knowledge contained in the 13th chapter of the Gita. We are there told, that humility (amanitvam) etc. constitute knowledge, and all the rest is ignorance. If this is true much that we hug to-day as knowledge is ignorance pure and simple, and therefore, only does us harm, instead of conferring any benefit. It makes the mind wander, and even reduces it to a vacuity, and discontent flourishes in endless ramifications of evil.

Needless to say, this is not a plea for inertia. Every moment of our life should be filled with activity, but that activity should be sattvika, tending to Truth. One, who has consecrated his life to service, cannot be idle for a single moment. But one has to learn to distinguish between good activity, and evil activity. This discernment goes naturally with a single-minded devotion to service.

Fearlessness

Every reader of the Gita knows that fearlessness heads the list of the Divine Attributes enumerated in the 16th chapter. Whether this is merely due to the exigencies of meter, or whether the pride of place has been deliberately yielded to fearlessness, is more than I can say. In my opinion, however, fearlessness richly deserves the first rank assigned to it there. For it is a sine qua non for the growth of the other noble qualities.

How can one seek Truth, or cherish Love, without fearlessness? As Pritam has it, 'the path of Hari (the Lord) is the path of the brave, not of cowards'. Hari here means Truth, and the brave are those armed with fearlessness, not with the sword, the rifle and other carnal weapons, which, strictly speaking are affected only by cowards.

Fearlessness connotes freedom from all external fear – fear of disease, bodily injury and death, of dispossession, of losing one's nearest and dearest, of losing reputation or giving offence, and so on. One, who overcomes the fear of death, does not surmount all other fears, as is commonly but erroneously supposed. Some of us do not fear death, but flee from the minor ills of life.

Some are ready to die themselves, but cannot bear their loved ones to be taken away from them. Some will swerve from the strait and narrow path simply because they are afraid of incurring the world's odium.

Excerpted from mkgandhi.org.

*   *   *

Section Ten

LOVE, COMPASSION

Osho compares Chaitanya Mahaprabhu with Mira and tilts the scales in favor of Chaitanya. Chaitanya was a great logician, renowned for his sharp mind and brilliant logic. Such a rational intellect was one day found singing and dancing through the streets of Navadeep. Meera, on the other hand, had nothing to do with logic. She was a loving woman; love was in her blood and bones. But Chaitanya was her opposite; he was not a man of love, and he turned to love and devotion – which was a miracle. This one-hundred-and-eighty degree turn in his life demonstrates the victory of love over logic.

Swami Viditatmananda Saraswati points out that the violence that takes place in nature is meant for survival. There is natural cruelty in animals that kill other animals. But it is not an unnecessary violence. There is a balance in nature that is maintained, such as ecological balance. Only man is capable of unnecessary violence and hence has a need to cultivate compassion. Animals are not cruel because they don't kill for the sake of killing, whereas, humans can kill for the sake of killing.

J. Krishnamurti links the problem of love with the problem called the mind. He claims it is the mind that destroys love. "Clever people, people who are cunning, do not know what love is because their minds are so sharp, because they are so clever, because they are so superficial – which means to be on the surface, and love is not a thing that exists on the surface." The mind seeks possession. But owning creates a barrier with regard to love. "If I own you, possess you, is that love," he asks.

*   *   *

Chaitanya Mahaprabhu

Chaitanya Mahaprabhu (1486-1534) was born in a Bengali Hindu family in the town of Nabadwip in Nadia, Bengal, India. In his youth, he was primarily known as an erudite scholar, whose learning and skills in argumentation in his locality were second to none. A number of stories also exist telling of Chaitanya's apparent attraction to the chanting and singing of Krishna's names from a very young age, but largely this was perceived as being secondary to his interest in acquiring knowledge and studying Sanskrit.

Chaitanya received the Gopala Krishna mantra as initiation from the ascetic Ishvara Puri. This meeting was to mark a significant change in Mahaprabhu's outlook from 'scholar' to 'devotee' and soon Chaitanya became the eminent leader of their Vaishnava group within Nadia.

After leaving Bengal and receiving entrance into the sannyasa order by Keshava Bharati, Chaitanya journeyed throughout the length and breadth of India for several years, chanting the divine Names of Krishna constantly. He spent the last 24 years of his life in Puri, Odisha, the great temple city of Jagannäth.

Osho

Acharya Rajneesh (1931–1990) later known as Osho was an Indian mystic, guru and spiritual teacher who has an international following. His syncretic teachings emphasize the importance of meditation, awareness, love, celebration, courage, creativity and humor: qualities which he viewed as suppressed by adherence to static belief systems, religious tradition and socialization. Rajneesh's teachings have had a notable impact on Western spirituality, as well as New Age thought, and their popularity has increased since his death.

The present excerpt is taken from the talks given by him on 'Krishna: The Man and His Philosophy' from 20/7/70 to 5/10/70 in Hindi in C.C.I. Chambers, Bombay. It is the most brilliant exposition and assessment of Krishna ever made.

37. Chaitanya demonstrates the victory of love over logic

Osho

Among the lovers of Krishna, Chaitanya Mahaprabhu's name is the most outstanding. There is a huge amount of literature on love in the form of poetry and epics and philosophical treatises. One can become knowledgeable about love, write great treatises on love, yet in reality he will not actually know what love is.

There is another person who has not read a word about love, but has experienced it, lived it. What is the difference between this man and the one who has gone through a huge pile of literature on love? This man knows love through experiencing; the other man knows it through words and concepts.

When Chaitanya says that unity and separateness of the world and God is beyond thought, he means much more than what meets the eye. Meera will say it is unthinkable, but she was never given to serious thinking – she was through and through a woman of feelings. But as far as Chaitanya is concerned, he was a great logician, renowned for his sharp mind and brilliant logic.

He had scaled the highest peaks of thinking. Pundits were afraid of entering into argument with him. He was incomparable as a debater; he had won laurel after laurel in philosophical discussions.

Such a rational intellect, who had indulged in hair splitting interpretations of words and concepts throughout his life, was one day found singing and dancing through the streets of Navadeep.

Meera, on the other hand, had never indulged in pedantry and scriptures; she had nothing to do with logic. She was a loving woman; love was in her blood and bones. So it was no wonder when she walked through the streets of Merta with a tanpoora in her hands, dancing and singing hymns of love. It was just natural.

But Chaitanya was her opposite; he was not a man of love, and he turned to love and devotion – which was a miracle. This one-hundred-and-eighty degree turn in his life demonstrates the victory of love over logic. He had defeated all his contemporaries with his logic, but when he came to himself he found it to be a self-defeating discipline. He came to a point where the mind lost and life and love won.

That is why among people who walked the path of Krishna, Chaitanya is simply extraordinary, incomparable. When I say so I am aware of Meera, who loves Krishna tremendously. But she does not come near Chaitanya. It is unthinkable how a tremendously logical mind like Chaitanya could come down from his ivory tower, take a drum in his hands, and dance and sing in the market place.

Can you think of Bertrand Russell dancing through the streets of London?

Chaitanya was like Russell – out and out intellectual. And for this reason his statement becomes immensely significant. He makes his statement that reality is unthinkable not with words, but with a drum in his hands – dancing and singing through the streets of his town, where he was held in great respect for his superb scholarship. It is in this way that he renounces mind, renounces thinking and declares that, "Reality is beyond thought, it is unthinkable."

Chaitanya's case demonstrates that they alone can transcend thinking who first enter into the very depth of thinking and explore it through and through.

Then they are bound to come to a point where thinking ends and the unthinkable begins.

This last frontier of mind is where a statement like this is born. That is why Chaitanya's statement has gathered immense significance; it comes after he crosses the last frontier of mentation. Meera never walked on that path; she came to love straight away. She cannot have the profundity of Chaitanya.

Excerpted from "Krishna: The Man and His Philosophy" with permission from OSHO International Foundation/www. osho.com.

* * *

Swami Viditatmanada Saraswati

Swami Viditatmanada Saraswati who was an engineer by profession, renounced the material world by taking sannyasa at the age of 44. He studied the Vedic scriptures and Sanskrit with his guru, Swami Dayananda Saraswati, and is a well known and highly respected teacher of Vedanta in both India and around the world.

Swami Viditatmananda is familiar with the lifestyles in India and the West, and has tremendous insight into both cultures. Swamiji spends most of his time teaching at Tattvatirtha Ashram in Ahmedabad as well as spending 3-4 months teaching at Arsha Vidya Gurukulam in Pennsylvania, U.S.A., which is the ashram founded by Swami Dayananda Saraswati. Swami Viditatmananda is also the Vice-President of that Institute.

An erudite scholar, Swamiji has dedicated his life to the spread of the ancient Vedic teachings pertaining to the knowledge of the Self. He imparts the core wisdom of the scriptures and explains each point in detail until he is sure that each person in front of him has understood. The depth of Swamiji's wisdom, compassion, and kindness brings great joy to all who come in contact with him.

Contact for details: www.avgsatsang.org

*   *   *

38. Compassion applies only to human beings

Swami Viditatmananda Saraswati

Question: Is compassion something that exists only in human beings?

Answer: Compassion applies only to human beings because only human beings can be cruel. The kind of violence that takes place in nature is meant for survival more than anything else. There is natural cruelty in animals that kill other animals. But it is not an unnecessary violence.

There is a balance in nature that is maintained, such as ecological balance.

So you find that there is no unnecessary violence in nature. Only man is capable of unnecessary violence and hence has a need to cultivate compassion. Animals are not cruel because they don't kill for the sake of killing, whereas, humans can kill for the sake of killing.

Q: Righteousness seems relative. What was not accepted 50 or 100 years ago seems perfectly acceptable today. What is right in one country or one faith is not right in another country or another faith.

151

Should what feels right to me be the only guideline to be followed for critical or difficult actions?

A: Righteousness is a universal value. However, what righteousness means in a given context needs to be interpreted. Values are universal and objective, but their interpretation is subjective and based on time, place, and condition. For example, we can talk of Arjuna's confusion regarding the battle. What may be right in the palace is not right in the battlefield. Arjuna asks, "How do you expect me to shower arrows at them when they should be worshipped with flowers?"

In this situation, both actions are right; in the palace, they are worthy of being worshipped with flowers, but in the battlefield they are worthy of being worshipped with arrows! The determination of the right relationship is also subject to interpretation. Therefore, values are universal, but their practice is particular or individual.

Righteousness also needs to be interpreted in today's context as opposed to that of 100 years ago. The interpretation of any value depending on the time, place, and condition calls for true maturity. Emotional maturity lies in being able to properly interpret a given value in a given situation.

Our practice, then, ultimately depends upon our interpretation alone. I may have the ability to interpret the truth, but how I interpret it decides what I do.

That will depend upon my maturity in interpreting what truth means.

Therefore, while in itself righteousness is not relative, its interpretation in a given situation is relative and depends upon factors such as the context, time, place, and condition.

Q: Why is animal sacrifice mentioned in the Vedas? Does it not go against the fundamental concept of non-violence?

A: I do not know why animal sacrifice is prescribed at all. Generally, a ritual has an overall effect; we do not know what each step generates. It is difficult to determine the effect of each individual step of a ritual. Even in the abhisekam that we do at the temple every day, we perform every step the way it is prescribed.

When animal sacrifice is prescribed as part of a ritual, it is not considered to be violence. Lord Buddha and Mahavir Jain protested against this aspect of the Vedic rituals. Basically, the Jain religion highlighted non-violence or ahimsä and Lord Buddha highlighted Compassion.

Excerpted from Arsha Vidya Gurukulam Memorial Day 2006 Camp satsanga, http://www.avgsatsang.org

* * *

J. Krishnamurti

Jiddu Krishnamurti (1895-1986) was born in Madanapalle, a small town in south India. He and his brother were adopted in their youth by Dr Annie Besant, then president of the Theosophical Society. Dr Besant and others proclaimed that Krishnamurti was to be a world teacher whose coming the Theosophists had predicted. To prepare the world for this coming, a world-wide organization called the Order of the Star was formed and the young Krishnamurti was made its head.

In 1929, however, Krishnamurti renounced the role that he was expected to play, dissolved the Order with its huge following, and returned all the money and property that had been donated for this work.

From then, for nearly sixty years, he travelled throughout the world talking to large audiences and to individuals about the need for a radical change in mankind. He is regarded globally as one of the greatest thinkers and religious teachers of all time. He belonged to no religious organization, sect or country, nor did he subscribe to any school of political or ideological thought. On the contrary, he maintained that these are the very factors that divide human beings and bring about conflict and war.

His teachings transcend man-made belief systems, nationalistic sentiment and sectarianism. At the same time, they give new meaning and direction to mankind's search for truth. His teaching, besides being relevant to the modern age, is timeless and universal.

Contact for details: www.jkrishnamurti.org

*   *   *

39. If I own you, possess you, is that love?

J. Krishnamurti

I do not think we shall understand the complex problem of love until we understand an equally complex problem which we call the mind. Have you noticed, when we are very young, how inquisitive we are? We want to know, we see many more things than older people.

We observe, if we are at all awake, things that older people do not notice. The mind, when we are young, is much more alert, much more curious, and wanting to know. That is why when we are young we learn so easily mathematics, geography.

As we grow older, our mind becomes more and more crystallized, more and more heavy, more and more bulky. Have you noticed in older people how prejudiced they are? Their minds are fixed, they are not open, they approach everything from a fixed point of view. You are young now, but if you are not very watchful, you will also become like that.

Is it not then very important to understand the mind and to see whether you cannot be supple, be capable of instant adjustments, of extraordinary capacities in every department of life, of deep research and understanding, instead of gradually becoming dull?

Should you not know the ways of the mind so as to understand the way of love? Because, it is the mind that destroys love. Clever people, people who are cunning, do not know what love is because their minds are so sharp, because they are so clever, because they are so superficial – which means to be on the surface, and love is not a thing that exists on the surface.

The mind says, "I think; it is mine; it is yours; I am hurt; I am jealous; I love; I hate; I am an Indian; I am a Muslim; I believe in this; I do not believe in that; I know; you do not know; I respect; I despise; I want; I do not want."

Your desire crystallizes your mind. Say, for example, I want to be a very rich man. The desire of wanting to be a wealthy man creates a pattern, and my thinking then gets caught in it, and I can only think in those terms.

Or, if I believe in something – in God, in communism, in a certain political system – the very belief begins to set the pattern because that belief is the outcome of my desire, and that desire strengthens the walls of the pattern.

Say, for example, I possess you as a wife or as a husband. Do you understand "possess"? You possess your saris or your coats, don't you? If somebody took them away, you would be angry, you would be anxious, you would be irritated. Why? Because you regard your saris or your coat or kurta as yours, your property; you possess it because through possession you feel enriched. Don't you?

Through having many saris, many kurtas, you feel rich, not only physically rich, but inwardly rich. So, when somebody takes your coat away, you feel irritated because inwardly you are being deprived of that feeling of being rich, that feeling of possession.

Owning creates a barrier, does it not, with regard to love. If I own you, possess you, is that love? I possess you as I possess a car, a coat, a sari, because in possessing, I feel very rich; I depend on it; it is very important to me inwardly.

This owning, this possessing, this depending, is what we call love. But if you examine it, you will see that behind it, the mind feels satisfied in possession. After all, when you possess a sari or many saris or a car or a house, inwardly it gives you a certain satisfaction.

Excerpted from the Ninth Talk at Rajghat, Varanasi, Dec 19, 1952. www.jkrishnamurti.org.

* * *

Section Eleven

MIND, EGO

Chuck Hillig has an explanation for the cosmic drama. You can't arrive at a place where you are already dwelling. Believing that you're not really there, however, provides the cosmic momentum for It to, seemingly, go out looking for Itself. "It's this purposeful misidentification that sets the entire drama of your life into (e) motion," he claims. "You can't use It (this philosophy) in everyday life because, actually, It will only be using you." His advice? Practice saying a resounding Yes! to whatever shows up for you.

Kabir used to teach by real life examples. Once a holy man claimed he saw Krishna dancing with gopis when he closed his eyes. Kabir asked him to catch hold of Krishna's hand next time he sees him. As the holy man tried to do so his eyes opened and he found he was holding his own hand. Kabir explained to him: "Mind is a powerful entity. Within moments it can cover distances far and wide. It can project the picture of whatever object or person one thinks of. But if you make it still, you can fetch precious gems of devotion from its depths."

Mahesh Yogi claims each one of us influences the universe for better or for worse. Giving an example, he says, "if we drop a stone in a pond, the ripples begin to move, and they move over the whole pond, reaching all the extremities. In the same way, every individual, by his every thought, word and action, shakes the entire universe." If the action of the individual is in conformity with the purpose of creation and the purpose of evolution, then all the great laws of nature readily serve the purpose of the individual.

Galen Sharp feels the mind is not a 'thing' or entity but a process. The thinking process. Simply a process that is happening automatically, the same as the heart is beating automatically. Everything happens by itself. Everything happens as it should. When the mind lets go of its sense of self and volition there is the deepest sense of complete peace and fulfillment. It is the Bliss spoken of by the ancient masters. The concept of being an individual is an invention of the mind.

*   *   *

Chuck Hillig

Chuck Hillig is a modern spiritual teacher, author and licensed psychotherapist whose clarity of expression has earned him the admiration and praise of many notable writers and lecturers in this area.

Chuck claims he was "born in Chicago in the last hundred years." Among the past positions he has held was that of Commissioned U.S. Naval Officer, Norfolk, Virginia.

Chuck writes personally and directly about the essence of non-dual spirituality and presents its astonishing truths to the average reader in ways that are totally unique, completely accessible and absolutely life-changing. Using his studies in both eastern philosophy and western psychology, Chuck's "Enlightenment Quartet" presents a world view that shows his readers how to fully live a truly enlightened and authentic life in the 21st Century by waking up to who they really are. Chuck Hillig makes his home in Locust Grove, Virginia.

Contact for details: www.chuckhillig.com

*   *   *

40. Ego-self can never experience Its own true nature

Chuck Hillig

When Consciousness pretends that there's a separation between what It says It is (the I), and what It says It isn't (the not-I), then the world mysteriously reappears. But It's not really going anywhere. Remember that the purpose of a song is not to arrive at the final note. The purpose of a song is found in the joyous singing of It. So it is with Consciousness. In other words, It's just singing!

Because Its simplicity is absolutely complete and pure, It can only manifest itself by pretending to be complex. In other words, when the indivisible Consciousness pretends to be divided into parts, It creates an illusory world of polarities. And you already are that very Consciousness, Itself!

This "you," (the illusory ego-self that you think you are), can never personally experience Its own true, fundamental nature. You can only be what It already is (i.e., It). In other words, you will never be able to get It simply because It already is It! Or, to put It another way, how can you ever arrive at a place where you are already dwelling?

Believing that you're not really there, however, provides the cosmic momentum for It to, seemingly, go out looking for Itself. It's this purposeful misidentification that sets the entire drama of your life into (e)motion.

You can't use It (this philosophy) in everyday life because, actually, It will only be using you. At one level, though, you can stay more aligned with It by consciously choosing exactly what It appears to be choosing for you. In other words, practice saying a resounding Yes! to whatever shows up for you. And, even when you feel like saying no, then just say yes to the fact that, at least for that moment, you're saying no.

It's best, though, to always make Yes! your default position in life. Don't reject anything, not even your own rejections!

Remember, however, that you, (the historical ego-self) are only pretending that you're able to manipulate or control It. Consciousness will always get its own way in the end, simply because, no matter where you think your ego-self is going, It is already there, waiting for you.

By definition, there can't be some of It here and then some more of It around the corner, too. That would be implying that It could, somehow, be divided from Itself. But, if It's absolutely simple and complete, then It can't really have any parts at all. It can only pretend to have parts. The you that you think you are is only one of the many parts that It is pretending to have.

So whatever is in your experience at this very instant is absolutely all of It.

There's really nothing and nowhere else.

Or, to put it another way, through Its own I's (your I's), It sees 100 percent of Itself, 100 percent of the time. None of It is ever missing simply because none of It can ever be left out. The idea of God doesn't come into It at all. God actually comes out of It. It is simply the ego's attempt to give a more formal name to the unnamable.

Excerpted from 'Frequently Asked Questions' on website http://www.chuckhillig.com

*   *   *

Kabir

Kabir, (1440-1518) a mystical poet and great saint of India, was born in Lahartara near the holy city Varanasi, India. He was never formally educated but his writings have greatly influenced Indian devotional movement. He celebrated the Divine which he saw everywhere and openly criticized all sects and the hypocrisy, pride and ignorant beliefs that kept people from the experience of Truth. He did so in the common language of the poor and at risk to his life from the orthodox Hindu Brahmins and the Muslim rulers of his day.

Kabir continues to remain spiritually significant to Hindus, Sikhs, and Muslims alike. The Sikhs have incorporated his poetry into their holy Granth Sahib and revere him as they do their ten Gurus. The songs of Kabir are known (and passionately performed) far and wide in India today.

Even the legend of his death speaks of interreligious reconciliation. The story goes that his Muslim and Hindu followers fought over his body and the burial rights. When the fighting factions opened the coffin, they found no body. Instead there were flowers inside. The Muslims buried half the flowers while the Hindus cremated the other half. Both sides viewed what happened as a miracle of divine intervention for religious reconciliation.

Contact for details: www.varanasi.org.in

41. Imagining of Krishna is only a trick of the mind: Kabir

V.K. Sethi

During one of his tours, Kabir is said to have met a holy man who claimed that whenever he closed his eyes and remembered Lord Krishna, he saw his deity dancing with the gopis, the milkmaids of Vrindavan. Kabir asked the sadhu to sit and do so in his presence.

The holy man closed his eyes and as he began to enjoy the dance, Kabir said, "When Krishna happens to come near you during the dance, catch hold of his hand and don't let it go."

The man at the first opportunity caught hold of the hand of Lord Krishna, who tried to release himself from the devotee's grip. In the struggle, the sadhu's eyes opened and he was amazed to see that he had firmly grasped his own hand. Bewildered and upset, the man looked at Kabir inquiringly.

Kabir said, "My good friend, do not be upset. What you have been seeing is a projection of your own mind. It is good that the illusion has broken." The holy man wanted to know more, and finding him in a receptive mood, Kabir explained to him further: "Mind is a powerful entity. Within moments it can cover distances far and wide. It can project the picture of whatever object or person one thinks of. More than the waves in the ocean are the waves of mind. But if you make it still, you can fetch precious gems of devotion from its depths."

Kabir continued: "If the one whom you saw was real, he would have talked with you, answered your questions and taken you to higher spiritual regions. You cannot visualize what you have never seen. If you try to and even succeed in seeing the object of your worship, it will only be the reflection of a mental image you have formed, not a reality. It will not respond to your actual spiritual needs."

Kabir had his own way of dealing with people. He would shock them in order to wake them from their stupor of religious superstition. A few accounts illustrate the radical ways that he would adopt to jolt those he chose to give enlightenment to. Jahan Gasht Shah, a Muslim dervish, had visited a number of places in India and met many holy men.

Having heard of Kabir as a great devotee, he came to Banaras to meet him. Learning of the fakir's arrival, Kabir said to one of his disciples that this man, though a noble soul and a true seeker of God, had not freed himself from certain deep-rooted prejudices which had become a hindrance in his spiritual progress. He asked the disciple to bring a pig and tie it near the door of his hut.

When Jahan Gasht came, he was scandalized to see a pig tied in front of Kabir's hut. Incensed, he turned back. Kabir, seeing him go, came out and called, "O Dervish, why do you go without seeing me?" Jahan Gasht stopped. "Kabir, I had heard that you were a pious man, but I find that you have kept an impure being at your door. I expected you to know the tenets better – your conduct befits only a kafir."

Kabir walked over to Jahan Gasht, greeted him with a salaam and said, "Friend, I have kept the impure one outside my house; you have given it shelter within your heart. Did not your eyes flash with anger and hatred for me? Are anger and hatred pure and within the tenets of religion?"

At Kabir's words, the dervish stood nonplused. Kabir took him by the hand and led him into the house. He explained to the fakir that in God's creation no being should be despised. How could one love God, if he had room for disdain and hatred in his heart?

Excerpted from 'Kabir The Weaver of God's Name,' Pages 27-28, Radha Soami Satsang Beas, Punjab, India

*   *   *

Maharishi Mahesh Yogi

Maharishi Mahesh Yogi (1918 –2008) was born Mahesh Prasad Varma in Jabalpur, Madhya Pradesh, India. He developed the Transcendental Meditation technique and was the leader and guru of a worldwide organization.

Mahesh Yogi became a disciple and assistant of Swami Brahmananda Saraswati, the Shankaracharya (spiritual leader) of Jyotirmath in the Himalayas.

In the 1970s, the Maharishi achieved fame as the guru to the Beatles and other celebrities. He started the TM-Sidhi program that claimed to offer practitioners the ability to levitate and to create world peace. In 1992 he moved to MERU, Holland, near Vlodrop, the Netherlands. In 2008, the Maharishi announced his retirement from all administrative activities and went into silence until his death three weeks later.

The Maharishi is reported to have trained more than 40,000 TM teachers and taught the Transcendental Meditation technique to "more than five million people."

Maharishi's Transcendental Meditation (TM) technique is easy to learn and enjoyable to practice. It is not a religion, philosophy or lifestyle. There are no lifestyle changes that need to be done. This simple, natural, effortless technique is practiced for 20 minutes twice each day while sitting comfortably with eyes closed.

Contact for details: www.maharishi.org, www.tm.org, in.tm.org

42. Individual and the cosmos are interdependent

Maharishi Mahesh Yogi

Our life is the expression of our inner potentialities. We project ourselves to the extent we know of our inner status, and there is much more to life than that which we are already living. Let us consider what more there is to life and what more can be lived than that we are living in the present. Certainly it is wise to know the whole extent of an expression of our life, and to try to bring in all that we have been missing so far.

We know, if we drop a stone in a pond, the ripples begin to move, and they move over the whole pond, reaching all the extremities. One slight stir in any part of the pond stirs the whole pond, influences the entire field of water and its surroundings. Similarly, by every thought, word, and action, every individual is setting forth influence in his surroundings, and that influence is not restricted to any boundaries. It goes on and on and reaches every level of creation.

Every individual, by his every thought, word and action, shakes the entire universe. This is the status of an individual. One is connected with the whole universe by every little bit of activity. An individual appears to be bound by the boundaries of home and by the boundaries of his own body, but in reality the subtle aspects of the individuality go to make universal existence. An individual is never an isolated individual. He is intimately interrelated with the whole cosmos.

Even more than that, he shares the responsibility for the life of the whole cosmos. The entire universe lies in the individual. Cosmic existence lies in the existence of the individual. Cosmic life rests in the individual life, and the individual life extends to cosmic life. The individual and the cosmos are interdependent. Neither of them is independent of the other.

Every move of the individual shakes the cosmos. The universe reacts to the individual action. Every individual has this power that shakes the universe, and shakes and saves the gods and angels in heaven. Man has this strength that upholds the universe. The individual, by his every action, serves the universe, and the great power of Nature is ready to serve the individual, if the individual influences the universe for the progression of the process of evolution.

By its very existence the creation is set in motion to go on and on through the steps of evolution. If the action of the individual is in conformity with the purpose of creation and the purpose of evolution, then the individual serves the cosmic purpose of life, and all the great laws of nature readily serve the purpose of the individual.

It is a simple and automatic process of give and take. As you sow, so shall you reap. When the individual behaves rightly he improves, and by so doing he contributes to the betterment of the entire universe; but when, knowingly or unknowingly, he behaves wrongly, he acts contrary to the process of evolution.

The laws of nature begin to react against him. The individual receives back the result of his wrong actions. He who will think right, speak good, and act truthfully, will receive the support of all the laws of nature carrying out the process of evolution around us.

We as the individuals have influence over the whole universe. Every one of us influences the entire universe by every little action we perform. Obviously, we do not perceive it, but at every moment we are either supporting or damaging the entire universe. Better we forget not the great responsibility that we can do and undo the entire creation that breathes the life of God, by the simple, individual mistakes of ours.

Excerpted from the transcript of a 1967 talk.

*   *   *

Galen Sharp

Sculptor and author Galen Sharp was born February 3, 1941 in Denver Colorodo, USA. Hectic travels and a successful career did not satisfy him. He became quite despondent but it eventually led him to deeply ponder the question, "What am I?" This culminated in an unexpected spontaneous mystical experience that completely redirected his life.

Galen developed a correspondence program based in these insights called "The Wholemind Intuitive Research Program", which drew thousands of members from all over the world. He also conducted seminars and workshops.

Several years ago Galen felt the need for a more private, simplified everyday life for himself and his family as well as a need to further deepen and mature this understanding. He withdrew from teaching and speaking and returned to school to obtain a degree in computer science and became an Oracle computer programmer.

His contact and learning with non-duality sage Wei Wu Wei (Terrence Stannus Gray) completely transformed his worldview and life.

His new book, 'What Am I? A Study in Non-Volitional Living' is about "the rare discovery that this world is not the "real world. And that "me" is not the "real me."

Contact for details: galensharp.com

43. The mind is not a 'thing' or entity but a process

Galen Sharp

You have never done anything! Because the mind has conceived itself to be an individual it also conceives of itself as the Thinker and also the 'Actor' or 'Doer'. Yet it is not anyone. The mind is not a 'thing' or entity but a process. The thinking process. Simply a process that is happening automatically, the same as the heart is beating automatically.

This is why we cannot live the perfect life even though we have been taught how a 'good' person should act. We know we shouldn't get angry at our spouse or our children whom we love, but despite the greatest resolve, we still do.

Why? Because we are not the thinker of our thoughts nor the doer of our actions. Because they are not our thoughts or our actions. We are not even the experiencer of the experience. What are we? We are what is perceiving the mind and that is not anyone.

We are what is perceiving the doing, but we are not the doer. We never were. We have never done the bad things and we have never done the good things either. Thoughts are affected by the environment (such as this article), inner habits and tendencies, and by the mind's concept of a 'me', but not by any actual 'me'.

We are incapable of interfering with the mind. Why? Because there is no one to interfere. We aren't anyone. Thus, we absolutely cannot have any volition. The concept of being an individual is an invention of the mind itself. It is an artifact of the way the mind works. The feeling of volition is an illusion spawned by this concept of 'me'.

We can never find our own will (volition) in any action. Every so called action is actually an automatic re-action of the mind with an accompanying feeling of volition. It is not 'me', it is the mind automatically going its own way! Simply watch the mind. Be aware of it. That's all that can be done because that is all we are doing right now.

That is all we ever do. That is all we have ever done. It is the mind that thinks and feels otherwise and we are what is aware of what the mind thinks and feels. We are perfectly open, empty and still. We are not in space or time. We can never be affected in any way. We have no needs or desires whatever. We just shine brilliantly, effortlessly.

We are what perceives what is appearing. In fact, it is because of this perceiving that anything at all appears. What we are is the beingness of what appears. The isness, or the am-ness, if you will of the very sense of 'I am'.

Another way to put it is that we are the Awareness in which everything appears (the here-now, the sense of presence, consciousness). See that we are simply and only the awareness of the mind while it goes its own way. Every sensation and feeling it has belongs to it, to manifestation. Not to ourself. With everything that appears in any way, we can say 'Not me, not me.'

We are the Watcher, or better yet the Watching, not the thinker, or the doer, or the experiencer. Once this is deeply and completely understood, the mind can let go of its sense of volition and its sense of being an individual, relax and just be.

Everything happens by itself. Everything happens as it should. Everything happens as it must. When the mind lets go of its sense of self and volition there is the deepest sense of complete peace and fulfillment. It is the Bliss spoken of by the ancient masters. All fear disappears.

Excerpted from 'An Exploration of Non-Volitional Living' as given on website www.galensharp.com

*   *   *

Section Twelve

MANIFESTATION, BODY

Paul Brunton points out that we live in a world whose fundamental law of being – as Buddha discovered and Jesus taught – is decay and death, change and transition. It was because they were so painfully aware of these truths that they sought and found the only *true* way of escape for man and that was into Nirvana – not into the physical body again. The animal part of us is doomed to oblivion, the spiritual part is ageless and deathless. And the physical body belongs to the animal part.

Greg Goode has a unique take on the body. He feels that in many nondual teachings, the body gets left out. Most of the attention goes to feelings and thoughts. And if the body is ignored, it will not be experienced as awareness, but rather as an unacknowledged container of awareness. Or simply a blind spot. This can create a sense of separation or alienation, as though the body were some sort of exception to the nondual investigation that examines other things. In the special investigation Goode conducts, the body is found to be nothing but the lightness and sweetness of awareness itself.

Swami Chidananda claims that the sacred scripture Ramacharita Manas, written by Tulasi Das, is Sri Rama Himself manifesting and expressing through the written word. On that particular Rama Navami Day, when Tulasidas started writing it, he says, the heavenly bodies presented the exact identical conjunctions and astronomical juxtapositions as were present upon the actual day of Sri Rama's Avatar upon earth, many thousands of years ago. Tulasi Das himself was fully aware of this fact and has stated, "whoever recites or listens to or sings the life story of the ornament of Raghu's Race (Rama) gets cleansed of all impurities."

Limitation is merely a state of consciousness. Hazrat Inayat Khan says those who are unhappy and dissatisfied with life and who make others unhappy, are those who are more limited while those who can help themselves and help others, who are happy and bring pleasure into the lives of others, are nearer to perfection. These are only conditions of the consciousness. When one is conscious of limitation, one is limited; when one is conscious of perfection, one is perfect.

*   *   *

Paul Brunton

Paul Brunton (1898-1981) was a British philosopher, mystic and traveler. He left a journalistic career to live among yogis, mystics, and holy men, and studied Eastern and Western esoteric teachings. Brunton is credited with introducing Ramana Maharshi to the West through his books *A Search in Secret India* and *The Secret Path*.

Brunton wrote eleven books. He also wrote daily thoughts in little notebooks, interviewed hundreds of teachers, fakirs, "fakers," and saints around the globe. While he discouraged people from becoming his followers, inevitably many who encountered him became students of his. For those fortunate individuals he offered his counsel and guidance.

As Brunton grew in spiritual stature, he was increasingly inclined towards anonymity, so much so that by the time he reached full illumination (the state known in India as "sahaja") in the early '60s he was practically forgotten by the public. He treasured the free and open circulation of the deepest, most precious teachings the world has to offer. To this end he committed his life to the task of creating a spiritual path suitable for the fast-paced world of the 21st century—a path that is outlined in *The Notebooks of Paul Brunton*.

Contact for details: www.paulbrunton.org

44. All attempts to perpetuate the body must fail

Paul Brunton

The treatment of unpleasant realities by not including them in his picture of the world comforts but at the same time befools a man. None of the great prophets like Jesus and Buddha denied the existence of sickness, the reality of pain, or the significance of suffering in the cosmos. No – they acknowledged them as being inseparable from human life but pitied the victims and offered them an inward comfort which was based on truth and reality.

The animal part of us is doomed to oblivion, the spiritual part is ageless and deathless. The physical body belongs to the animal part. All attempts to perpetuate it must fail and arise from confusing the two levels of being, the transient and the eternal . . . .

People ask why, if all is mind, if – as you say – our bodies are only ideas, can we not control regulate and improve our bodies by controlling regulating and improving our minds? Why not go further still, with Christian Science, and play with the possibility, not only of these achievements, but also of rendering the body immortal by thinking it so?

The answer is that nobody can deny the creative power of the mind. It may do all these things, except the last. That it will never do. Why? Because we live in a world whose fundamental law of being – as Buddha discovered and Jesus taught – is decay and death, change and transition.

Indeed, it was because they were so painfully aware of these truths that they sought and found the only *true* way of escape for man and that was into Nirvana, into the Kingdom of Heaven – not into the physical body again! No Christian Scientist from the first founder down to the latest follower has ever achieved physical immortality, nor ever will.

"Man will never tire of seeking immortality," wrote Dr. Alexis Carrel, whose biological researches, yet mystical sympathies, entitle him to speak with high authority. "He will not attain it, because he is bound by certain laws of his organic constitution . . . . Never will he vanquish death. Death is the price he has to pay for his brain and his personality."

Now as for the other things, the possibilities of spiritual healings of pathological conditions, miraculous mental cures of disease, and rapid acceleration of organic repairs through concentrated thinking, I repeat that we do not deny them. They have always existed, always been demonstrated.

The relation between psychological and physical processes must certainly exist if our doctrine is true. But there are two other factors at work in human life which must also be considered and must not be ignored. What are they? The first is the factor of destiny, self-earned in previous lives and now awaiting physical expression in the present life. It has something to say, whether we like it or not.

The second is the factor of renunciation. When you accept the doctrine that all is mind and each individual thing is but an ephemeral idea, you must perforce accept the doctrine that you as an individual, as the ego, are also an ephemeral idea.

Now when you go further and declare that you want reality, you want to find eternal and not ephemeral life, you will have to abandon the fleeting idea for the eternal Mind in which it occurs: that is, you will have to sink the ego and merge its will in the greater universal will of the Infinite Being.

Do this! What will you find next? That your personal desires have sunk with it, that your individual wishes and hopes and fears have dissolved and disappeared. The desire for bodily betterment, however very attractive, would have gone too. You cannot have a single desire and yet enter the Kingdom of Heaven, as Jesus pointed out . . .

Reprinted from the Paul Brunton Notebooks, Category 10 Healing of the Self, Chapter 1: The Laws of Nature #35 and # 37 with permission from the Paul Brunton Philosophic Foundation www.PaulBrunton.org

* * *

Greg Goode

Greg Goode is a Doctor of Western philosophy as well as a self-realized teacher of Advaita and Buddhism and is equally at home with all approaches. After studying Psychology at California State University, Greg studied philosophy in Cologne, Germany, and received his M.A. and Ph.D. in Philosophy from the University of Rochester

Greg sees straight to the heart of a problem and explains the solution with insight, clarity and humor. Since 1996 Greg has been a philosophical counselor in New York, where he also holds satsangs.

Before becoming enlightened Greg described himself as feeling a deep sense of loneliness, alienation, lack of fulfillment, and a strong yearning from the heart and mind to know "What is it all about? What is the purpose of life? He tried many different paths.

Greg's answer came one day while he was reading a book about consciousness, and when the answer came, it didn't come as a conceptual statement like "It is ABC." Rather, it came by way of the world and the body imploding into a brilliant light, and the willing, phenomenal self-thinning out, disappearing in a blaze of the same light.

Contact for details: www.heartofnow.com

* * *

45. The body is nothing other than awareness

Greg Goode

The nurse comes in and says, "Doctor, there's an invisible man here for an appointment." The doctor says, "Tell him I can't see him."

—Overheard in a doctor's office

The body seems to be part of the world. But it also seems to be that which perceives and feels the world. And it seems to be where we are localized.

The way we normally think of the body, it seems to be a physical object.

But unlike a table or car, the body seems to be endowed with sentience.

The body can perceive. It can feel pleasure and pain. The body contains the mind – and some people would say that there is no "mind" strictly speaking, but that it's the brain which is programmed to do everything that is called thinking.

The body seems to be the locus of a vast function of consciousness. The body seems to be where "I" am localized. We think, "Maybe rocks and trees are able to see and feel too, but my own body and the ability to see and feel all seem bundled up into one. This body certainly seems to be where I am!" It seems as though I come and go with the body. And it seems that I began when the body began, and that I will cease when the body ceases.

In this part we'll explore the body. This is of paramount importance in one's investigation into one's nature. In many nondual teachings, the body gets left out. For various reasons, most of the attention goes to feelings and thoughts. But if the body is not explored in a direct way, then there will still remain a sense of localization and identity that seems rooted in the body.

If the body is ignored, it will not be experienced as awareness, but rather as an unacknowledged container of awareness. Or simply a blind spot. This can create a sense of separation or alienation, as though the body were some sort of exception to the nondual investigation that examines other things.

Even the thoughts and feelings that are examined and loosened up in nondual teachings can carry a subtle quality where they seem to be arising "here," which translates into a spatial designation.

And, of course, if there's a "here," then there is also a "not here," which is a very sticky dualism. When we investigate the body, we will see in different ways that the body is nothing but the lightness and sweetness of awareness itself. Whether experience seems to be orgasmic pleasure or intense pain, direct experience discovers nothing to the body other than the clarity and freedom of awareness. The body is not the container or conduit for awareness. The body doesn't perceive awareness. The body just is awareness.

We will explore the body in three ways, and in each of these ways, we will discover that our direct experience is that the body is nothing other than awareness.

As An Object

First, we'll investigate the body as another case of a physical object, just as we investigated the world. We will discover that the body doesn't sense, but arises as sensations, the same way a table or an orange does. We have already seen how these "sensations" are nothing other than witnessing awareness.

As A Feeler

Next, we'll investigate the body as something that seems to feel. It seems to feel when objects (including the body itself) touch it. We will investigate pains, pleasures, itches, twitches, movements and the sense of the body being located in a place. We'll discover that in direct experience there is no evidence that these experiences are felt by a body or in a body. We'll discover that these experiences, as well as the body itself, are nothing other than witnessing awareness.

As A Container of Awareness

Finally, we'll investigate the sense that the body contains awareness. This includes the sense that there seems to be an inside and an outside to the body, and we seem to be on the inside.

Excerpted from The Direct Path, by Greg Goode, pp. 68-70, published by Non-Duality Press

*   *   *

Swami Chidananda Saraswati

Swami Chidananda Saraswati (1916-2008) was born Sridhar Rao in Karnataka where he grew up in an atmosphere of discipline and spiritual devotion. In 1938 he graduated with distinction from the Christian Loyola College of Madras. There he imbibed the virtues of Jesus' love, compassion and humility, and realized that the Bible was "just as living and real as the words of the Vedas, the Upanishads and the Bhagavad-Gita".

In 1943 he came to his master Swami Sivananda, the founder of the Sivananda Ashram and the Divine Life Society, in Rishikesh. In 1949, he was initiated into sannyasa diksha and was appointed General Secretary of the institution. Swami Sivananda recognized in him the natural and unusual qualities of "a jivanmukta, a great saint, an ideal yogi, a parabhakta and a jnani."

In 1963, after the mahasamadhi of Swami Sivananda, Swami Chidananda was made President of the Divine Life Society which he helped develop through his selfless service, untiring energy and extensive travels all over the country and abroad. He was the motto of the Society incarnate — "Serve, love, meditate, realize" — and remained all his life a simple monk despite being a world renowned spiritual teacher.

Contact for details: www.sivanandaonline.org

46. 'Tulasi Ramayan a manifestation of Ram himself'

Swami Chidananda

Tulasi-Ramayana, popularly known as Ramacharita-Manas, was started by Tulasidas upon one Sri Rama Navami Day, and it is said that on that particular Rama Navami Day, the heavenly bodies presented the exact identical conjunctions and astronomical juxtapositions as were present upon the actual day of Sri Rama's Avatar upon earth, many thousands of years ago.

Thus it may be said that in the birth of this inspiring and life-transforming poetical work of the great Tulasi Das, we have a reincarnation of that very divinity (this time in a different form) as appeared in the person of Lord Rama previously.

The sacred Ramacharita Manas is, therefore, Bhagavan Sri Rama Himself manifesting and expressing through the written word. Tulasi Das himself was fully aware of this fact, for he states in unmistakable terms: "That man who recites or listens to or sings the life story of the ornament of Raghu's Race (Rama) gets cleansed of all impurities of this Iron Age and without difficulty attains straight-away to the divine abode of Lord Rama."

Study of this rare treasure is, therefore, like a dip in the transcendental ocean of Satchidananda itself. It is a nectarine lake bathing in which you attain freedom from all afflictions and casting aside the shackles of birth and death, you rise up into the realm of eternal bliss and immortality. Hail, all Hail, to the divine Ramacharita-Manas. All glory be unto its saintly author.

The life of this great saint is filled with a number of inspiring incidents which come as a flood of light revealing to us certain lofty truths of spiritual life. Upon one occasion the jealous enemies of the saintly Tulasi Das wished to destroy the precious manuscripts then being written day-by-day, by the saint.

They hired two murderous ruffians for this purpose, who were to break into the house of Tulasi Das at dead of night and bring away the manuscripts. When these fierce felons had gained entrance into his abode on a dark night and were stealthily moving towards the altar wherein the manuscripts reposed, lo, two shining youths with blazing eyes and angered looks confronted them with drawn bows wherein glittered sharp and deadly arrows ready poised to spring forth upon the midnight marauders and make quick end of them, then and there. The ruffians were struck down with fear.

They cry out in terror, run up to the sleeping saint and fall at his feet entreating him to protect their lives. They cry: "Oh, sire, save us, oh, save us from these wrathful, young warriors with terrific looks." Thus, it was that in the life of this great saint a tangible presence and the ever-protecting hand of the Lord was a living fact.

Similarly did the divine presence come visibly to his aid, when the then emperor tried to persecute the saint. Lord Hanuman assuming innumerable forms so devastated the capital that the emperor had to come to his knees and ask pardon of saint Tulasi Das. The declaration of the Lord in the Gita that he ever abides by those, who constantly think of Him is practically demonstrated in the experience of Tulasi Das.

Excerpted from the lecture 'Tulasidas' Gift to Humanity.' www.dlhq.org

*   *   *

Hazrat Inayat Khan

Inayat Khan (1882 – 1927) was the founder of The Sufi Order in the West in 1914 (London) and teacher of Universal Sufism. He came to the West as a Northern Indian classical musician, having received the honorific "Tansen" from the Nizam of Hyderabad, but he soon turned to the introduction and transmission of Sufi thought and practice. His message of divine unity (Tawhid) focused on the themes of love, harmony and beauty. He taught that blind adherence to any book rendered religion void of spirit. Branches of Inayat Khan's movement can be found in the Netherlands, France, England, Germany, the United States, Canada, Russia and Australia.

Hazrat was born in Vadodara, Gujarat, to a noble family, as on his paternal side (made of mystics and poets) he descended from Pashtuns of Afghanistan initially settled in Sialkot, Punjab.

In 1910 he came to the West, traveling first as a touring musician and then as a teacher of Sufism, visiting three continents. Eventually he married Ora Ray Baker, a second-cousin of Christian Science founder Mary Baker Eddy. Khan returned to India in 1926 and there chose the site of his tomb, the Nizamuddin Dargah complex in Delhi.

Contact for details: http://www.hazrat-inayat-khan.org

*　　*　　*

47. **Limitation is merely a condition of Consciousness**

Hazrat Inayat Khan

The process of going from limitation to perfection is called mysticism.

Mysticism means developing from limitation to perfection. All pain and failure belong to limitation; all pleasure and success belong to perfection. In one's own surroundings, one will find that those who are unhappy and dissatisfied with life and who make others unhappy, are those who are more limited; those who can help themselves and help others, who are happy and bring pleasure into the lives of others, are nearer to perfection.

What is meant by limitation and what by perfection? These are only conditions of the consciousness. When one is conscious of limitation, one is limited; when one is conscious of perfection, one is perfect. Because he who is limited in the limited consciousness is the same as he who is perfect in the perfect consciousness.

To give an example: there was a son of a rich man who had plenty of money put in his name in the bank. But he did not know this; and when he wished to spend some money he found very little in his pocket. This made him limited. In reality his father had put a large sum in the bank, but he was not conscious of it. It is exactly the same with every soul.

Every soul is conscious of what it possesses and is unconscious of what is put in its name. What is within one's reach, one feels to be one's own, but what does not seem to be within one's reach one considers to be outside.

This is natural. But wisdom opens a door to look out and see if that which seems outside is not meant to be known too.

Sometimes the mastery of life is known to a person; he may not be a mystic, but if his time comes, he knows it. One day I was interested when a man, who had done nothing but business all his life and made himself so rich that he was perhaps one of the richest men in the country, wanted to show me his park, a beautiful park he had around his house.

While I was his guest we were taking a walk. He said, 'It is wonderful to come here into my park in the morning and evening.' I asked him, 'How far does your park extend?' And he said, 'Do you want to know? Do you see the horizon from here?' I said, 'Yes.' He told me, 'All this land is mine and the sea besides. All that you can see.'

It was a wonderful answer, and an example of the theory I have mentioned; he was not only conscious of what he possessed, but of all that was there. He did not make a dividing line between what was his own and what was beyond.

It is a mystery, and it is difficult for anyone to look at life in this way. But this man who was in business, this man who never even thought of mysticism, could also arrive at that conception which the mystic discovers after years of meditation. It was a purely mystical conception.

When dervishes, who sometimes have patched sleeves or are scantily clad, who sometimes have food and sometimes not, address one another, they say, 'O King of Kings, O Emperor of Emperors'. It is the consciousness of what is king or emperor which is before them. The boundary of their kingdom is not limited. The whole universe is their kingdom.

It is in this way that a soul proceeds towards perfection, by opening the consciousness and raising it higher. When the soul evolves spiritually, it rises to a height where it sees a wider horizon; therefore its possession becomes greater.

Excerpted from chapter 'Mastery' in 'Mental Purification and Healing, The Sufi Message, Vol IV'

*   *   *

Section Thirteen

SCIENCE

Jeff Warren says that scientific exploration is now turning inward. Investigating sleep he says it is a misconception to believe that we lose consciousness when the lights go out. At night consciousness just turns inside out. Instead of moving through a world constructed from sensory input, we move through a world constructed from memory and imagination. Another surprising thing he discovered was that expectations play a big role in not just shaping experience but in actually provoking specific brain activity. This he finds mind-boggling and revolutionary.

James Swartz once asked his guru, Swami Chinmayananda, how does he claim that Vedanta is a science and not a religion. Chinmayananda told him, "In science you have certain theories that have to be proven by experiment before they can be accepted as knowledge. Vedanta presents the theory that there is a God, which we call the self, and it provides methods for verifying the truth of that theory. If they are used properly, the practices and techniques will deliver the experience and knowledge of God. Religion however asks that you merely believe in the existence of something you cannot practically verify."

Paramhansa Yogananda relates how his guru was disappointed on his visit to Kumbha Mela in Allahabad where in the clamor and surge of the crowd he saw no illumined face of a master. He felt Western scientists working for the practical good of mankind should be more pleasing to God than "these idlers who profess religion but concentrate on alms." His guru admonished him saying, "Everything on earth is of mixed character, like a mingling of sand and sugar. Be like the wise ant which seizes only the sugar, and leaves the sand untouched. Though many sadhus here still wander in delusion, yet the *mela* is blessed by a few men of God-realization.' He recommended East and West joining each other to establish a golden middle path of activity and spirituality combined.

*   *   *

Jeff Warren

Jeff Warren is a Toronto-born (1971) journalist and meditation teacher and author of The Head Trip: Adventures on the Wheel of Consciousness. At school, he was "a disregulated partier," and it was only after he developed ADD in the wake of a massive brain injury – high on psilocybin mushrooms in his final year, he fell 30 feet out of a tree – that he became fascinated by what he calls "all these flavors of consciousness that people aren't really aware of."

One of the flavors that most intrigued him was at the centre of many meditative practices—what he called "a raw, undiluted substrate to conscious experience that forms the backdrop to everything else." Warren began to dabble in Buddhist meditation which helped relieve his chronic neck pain.

A week-long retreat in Scotland in 2005, however, was even more epiphanic. Warren realized that meditation was "a dignified attempt to come to grips with being human with the resources you have right there. Not depending on some guru, or some drug, or some psychotherapy. Just a very simple technique that, repeated again and again and again, will eventually change the way you relate to the world at the deepest level."

Contact for details: www.jeffwarren.org

48. Scientific exploration is now turning inwards

Jeff Warren

This is going to sound hyperbolic but I really believe we're at the dawn of a new age of scientific exploration. The external world is mapped; now the explorers are turning inward. The galleons have left port. They're approaching a huge mysterious continent. They won't be the first to arrive. There are paths already cut in the forest, where shamans and monks and others have set up outposts and launched their own expeditions into the interior.

It's a thrilling story, a lurid epic in the making, and yet almost no one has any idea it's happening.

As far as our misconceptions about sleep, I would say the biggest one is this idea that we lose consciousness when the lights go out. This couldn't be further from the truth. At night consciousness just turns inside out. Instead of moving through a world constructed from sensory input, we move through a world constructed from memory and imagination.

We do lose certain self-reflective properties, and – critically – our short-term memories are compromised so we don't remember many of our experiences. But when you wake people up in the night most of them report some kind of mental activity – either the strange snap-shot narratives of sleep onset, the fully immersive dreams of REM, or the low-level "mentation" of deep sleep. Even in the emptiest bliss-saturated realms of slow wave sleep the experiencing self remains. Consciousness is 24-hours.

What surprised you the most about brains (or about your brain)?

It's mind I find most surprising. RE: brains, I would say the most surprising thing I learned was about the role expectations – a big mind culprit – play not just in shaping experience but in actually provoking specific brain activity. This gets into the whole placebo thing which is also mind-boggling and revolutionary. My guess is placebo will be another big theme in the New World explorations.

Were there any cherished beliefs about brains (your brain) that you had to relinquish?

I guess my world-weary evolutionary psychology outlook – about the hardwired inevitability of our modular mental inheritances – that pretty much got blown out of the water while researching the book. Now I think the sociobiologists are the cavemen. More interesting than the evolutionary story, to me, is the fresher and more nuanced story of how our neuro-plastic brains interact with our mongrel-fantastic culture.

You largely avoid the question of drugs and altered consciousness

I'm interested in drug-induced alternations of consciousness, but my feeling is they're the really obvious shit. Too many "investigators of consciousness" overlook the fine-grained shifting texture of day-to-day consciousness. It's the difference between the big budget Hollywood blockbuster and the art house Henry James adaptation.

Drug-induced alterations of consciousness have great CGI – which is fine, I mean who doesn't appreciate form constant explosions and DMT Machine Elves? – the problem is, character development sucks, or rather, the characters – and by characters I mean the objects of consciousness – tend to be cartoons.

They're exaggerated, that's what psychedelics do – "non-specific amplifiers" Stanislav Grof calls them. They expand the whole topography of the mind. It's possible more than this is going on but that's another story.

Jeff Warren is the author of 'The Head Trip: Adventures on the Wheel of Consciousness.' *This excerpt is taken from an interview with website Bookslut.*

*   *   *

James Swartz

James Swartz was born in Butte, Montana, USA. in 1941. He grew up in Lewiston, Idaho. Six months short of graduation he ran off to Hawaii to start a successful business. But something was terribly wrong; at 26 he had become an alcoholic, chain smoking gluttonous adulterer and life in every respect was not worth living. One day in the Post Office in Waikiki he had a life changing epiphany that put him on the path to freedom.

Today James is a traditional Vedanta teacher, a dyed-in-the-wool Shankara Vedantin who has been studying and teaching scripture for forty years, since his self-realization in his late twenties under the discipleship of Swami Chinmayananda in India.

James has developed a passion for de-mystifying Vedanta for a Western audience. He has written many short books on Vedanta including What is Advaita, Tattva Both, Atma Both, Mandukya Upanishad, Narada Bhakti Sutra, Bhagavad Gita, Panchadasi and The Kathopanishad.

James travels the world to teach, and still spends a good part of every year teaching in India. In his video series, he explains in plain English the complex discoveries of the Rishis in a simple down-home manner that has delighted his students throughout the years.

Contact for details: www.shiningworld.com

*   *   *

49. Vedanta is not a religion, it is a science

James Swartz

I believe the conviction arising from legitimate spiritual experiences induced by drugs . . . that there is something beyond the realm of the senses and the mind's mad craving for pleasure and security . . . not drugs themselves, is the most enduring and important legacy of the Sixties and forms the basis of a spiritual revolution that continues today.

In any case, a week before we arrived a psychologist, vowing not to move until he attained enlightenment, locked himself in a cabin and began meditating. A few days later, alerted by his screams, the authorities broke in and hauled him off to the state insane asylum a few miles down the road.

"It is dangerous to take this sort of an attitude," said the Swami (Chinmayananda) of the incident. "Enlightenment does not come simply because you want it. You have to be prepared. This is why in our country we have the guru-disciple lineage. The disciple must cultivate the requisite ethical and moral standards, a keen sense of discrimination, dispassion, and a calm mind. And he should have a teacher, someone who has already successfully walked the path. This is typical of the independent and egocentric approach to life in America."

"Why is it a science?" I asked one afternoon. "It seems more like a religion."

"It is a science in this sense," he replied. "In science you have certain theories that have to be proven by experiment before they can be accepted as knowledge. Vedanta presents the theory that there is a God, which we call the self, and it provides methods for verifying the truth of that theory. If they are used properly, the practices and techniques will deliver the experience and knowledge of God."

"Religion asks that you merely believe in the existence of something you cannot practically verify," he continued. "You are promised release later on in heaven, but the idea of actually knowing God intimately and directly as your own self is considered blasphemy. Our idea is that God must be of practical use. Faith alone is not enough. We want to experience God, to live in the God as God. Only then can we accept the theory of God's existence, which at that time is no longer a theory, but knowledge."

"Of course God can never die, but God has died here because faith has killed Him. If you believe God can only be known through faith, you rob yourself of the here-and-now experience of God."

"The West has the idea that the physical universe is reality and that it is made up of matter only. And consciousness supposedly comes out of matter. To us this is a ridiculous idea because matter is insentient. How can sentiency, Consciousness, come out of matter? Vedanta says that the universe is Consciousness from the very beginning. In fact, before the beginning. It does not evolve once the material universe gets to a certain stage. Even if it did how would the universe evolve without Consciousness? Evolution, any kind of change, implies Consciousness or energy."

"So you think that the only reality is the material world and you explore that.

The way you explore it is called science. And you have been very successful in exploring and explaining it using the scientific method. We do not quarrel with you on this point. In practical ways your use of science has exceeded ours. This is why your standard of living is much better than ours.

"But long before there was a Western civilization our sages were exploring the inner world, the world of mind or consciousness with a scientific mentality. So over thousands of years we have developed a proven subjective science. It is not just theories. It is not the opinion or system of some brilliant man, like Nietzsche or Sartre or Freud, or religious dogma, but the accumulated knowledge and experience of tens of thousands of subjective scientists."

Excerpted from 'Mystic by Default'

*   *   *

Paramahansa Yogananda

Paramahansa Yogananda (1893 – 1952) was an Indian yogi and guru who introduced millions of westerners to the teachings of meditation and Kriya Yoga through his book, *Autobiography of a Yogi.*

Yogananda was born Mukunda Lal Ghosh in Gorakhpur, Uttar Pradesh, India to a devout family. His quest for a spiritual master ended when he met Swami Yukteswar Giri, in 1910, at the age of 17. In 1915, he took formal vows into the monastic order and became 'Swami Yogananda Giri'.

In 1920, Yogananda went to the United States to attend an International Congress of Religious Liberals. There he founded the Self-Realization Fellowship (SRF) to disseminate worldwide his teachings on India's ancient practices and philosophy of Yoga and its tradition of meditation.

He lectured and taught and established an international center for Self-Realization Fellowship in Los Angeles, California, which became the spiritual and administrative heart of his growing work. Yogananda lived in US from 1920–1952, interrupted by a trip to India in 1935–1936 to visit his guru.

The last four years of his life were spent primarily in seclusion with some of his inner circle of disciples at his desert ashram in Twenty-nine Palms, CA.

Contact for details: www.yogananda-srf.org

50. India & West have to learn much from each other

Paramhansa Yogananda

The religious fairs held in India since time immemorial are known as *Kumbha Melas;* they have kept spiritual goals in constant sight of the multitude. Devout Hindus gather by the millions every six years to meet thousands of sadhus, yogis, swamis, and ascetics of all kinds. Many are hermits who never leave their secluded haunts except to attend the *melas* and bestow their blessings on worldly men and women.

"I was not a swami at the time I met Babaji," Sri Yukteswar went on. "But I had already received *Kriya* initiation from Lahiri Mahasaya. He encouraged me to attend the *mela* which was convening in January, 1894 at Allahabad. It was my first experience of a *kumbha;* I felt slightly dazed by the clamor and surge of the crowd. In my searching gazes around I saw no illumined face of a master. Passing a bridge on the bank of the Ganges, I noticed an acquaintance standing near-by, his begging bowl extended.

"'Oh, this fair is nothing but a chaos of noise and beggars,' I thought in disillusionment. 'I wonder if Western scientists, patiently enlarging the realms of knowledge for the practical good of mankind, are not more pleasing to God than these idlers who profess religion but concentrate on alms.'

"My smoldering reflections on social reform were interrupted by the voice of a tall sannyasi who . . ." who took me to a "tree whose branches were sheltering a guru with an attractive group of disciples. The master, a bright unusual figure, with sparkling dark eyes, rose at my approach and embraced me.

"'Welcome, Swamiji,' he said affectionately.

"'Sir,' I replied emphatically, 'I am *not* a swami.'

"'Those on whom I am divinely directed to bestow the title of "swami" never cast it off.' The saint addressed me simply, but deep conviction of truth rang in his words.

"Babaji – for it was indeed he – motioned me to a seat near him under the tree.

"'What do you think of the *Kumbha Mela*?'

"'I was greatly disappointed, sir.' I added hastily, 'Up until the time I met you. Somehow saints and this commotion don't seem to belong together.'

"'Child,' the master said, though apparently I was nearly twice his own age, 'for the faults of the many, judge not the whole. Everything on earth is of mixed character, like a mingling of sand and sugar. Be like the wise ant which seizes only the sugar, and leaves the sand untouched. Though many sadhus here still wander in delusion, yet the *mela* is blessed by a few men of God-realization.'

"In view of my own meeting with this exalted master, I quickly agreed with his observation.

"'Sir,' I commented, 'I have been thinking of the scientific men of the West, greater by far in intelligence than most people congregated here, living in distant Europe and America, professing different creeds, and ignorant of the real values of such *melas* as the present one. They are the men who could benefit greatly by meetings with India's masters. But, although high in intellectual attainments, many Westerners are wedded to rank materialism. Others, famous in science and philosophy, do not recognize the essential unity in religion. Their creeds serve as insurmountable barriers that threaten to separate them from us forever.'

"'I saw that you are interested in the West, as well as the East.' Babaji's face beamed with approval. 'I felt the pangs of your heart, broad enough for all men, whether Oriental or Occidental. That is why I summoned you here.

"'East and West must establish a golden middle path of activity and spirituality combined,' he continued. 'India has much to learn from the West in material development; in return, India can teach the universal methods by which the West will be able to base its religious beliefs on the unshakable foundations of yogic science.

Excerpted from the Autobiography of a Yogi, Chapter 36, entitled 'Babaji's Interest in the West'

*　　*　　*

INDEX

Index